MW01535827

Youth and Substance Abuse

Kathryn Daley

Youth and Substance Abuse

palgrave
macmillan

Kathryn Daley
RMIT University,
Melbourne, Victoria, Australia

ISBN 978-3-319-33674-9   ISBN 978-3-319-33675-6   (eBook)
DOI 10.1007/978-3-319-33675-6

Library of Congress Control Number: 2016956413

Cover illustration: © Johner Images / Alamy Stock

Printed on acid-free paper

This Palgrave Macmillan imprint is published by Springer Nature
The registered company is Springer International Publishing AG
The registered company address is: Gewerbestrasse 11, 6330 Cham, Switzerland

For my family: my brother Jared and our mother, Lorraine
I wish you were here.
And for Chris Chamberlain.

Acknowledgements

I hope as researchers you continue to wonder about those unrevealed stories. Not just because they are interesting, but because they are unjust.

At the beginning of this research, a woman who had been raised in state care anonymously left this comment on my blog. Her voice has kept me focused and I thank her. Undertaking studies of the vulnerable is voyeuristic in nature but that should not be its primary aim. Although this research was not a pleasant undertaking, it was a very fulfilling endeavour. My interest in research arose after observing an absence of studies that explained the biographies of young people experiencing chronic issues with drug use and homelessness. It was always hoped to have this project published, to "reveal" their stories, to make public the injustices some face.

The 73 young people who participated in both this study and its pilot were an endless source of inspiration—I hope that I do you justice. Gratitude is also extended to my former clients who gave me the insights that sparked my passion and who encouraged me to tell their story.

I extend much appreciation to the staff at the Youth Support + Advocacy Service (YSAS) and Barwon Youth Alcohol and Other Drug Service for their time, assistance and support. I particularly thank Salli Hickford, Josie Taylor, David Murray and Andrew Bruun. Many thanks are also due to Professors Robert MacDonald and Tim Newburn, who examined the original thesis this work stemmed from—their feedback was most helpful. In addition to this, the anonymous reviewer sourced through Palgrave - who I have since learned was Professor Shane Blackman - must also be thanked publicly. As an early-career researcher it was wonderful to receive such constructive and helpful feedback that improved the final output.

The Australian government provided me with free tuition as well as a scholarship to undertake this study, which was a privilege for which I am most grateful. The costs associated with fieldwork were supplemented by a grant from the Foundation for Alcohol Research and Education (FARE). In addition to this financial support, I received wonderful kindness and collegiality from staff in the School of Global, Urban and Social Studies, and Centre for Applied Social Research, especially Associate Professor Guy Johnson, Professor Pavla Miller and Dr Helen Marshall.

Assistance in the intellectual development of this work was not the only assistance required to see its fruition. This research was bookended with the deaths of my brother and mother. While the project gave me a sense of purpose in a time where purpose may otherwise have been difficult to summon, I am deeply indebted to a community of very special people who, in various practical and nurturing ways, supported me: Melissa, Matthew, Memphis and Cooper Pace, John and Sue Hancock, Maureen Gibbens, Russell van Sanden, Shani Pearce, Geoffrey Mead, Erin Gamble, Madeline Hallwright, Andrew McLean and Krystle Gatt-Rapa—words are inadequate, but thank you.

Professor Chris Chamberlain—my "Tyrant"—has been my ally, my harshest critic and my pseudo-parent (under the guise of "Supervisor"). It is certain that I would not have begun this research without your (forceful) suggestion, but it is equally certain that I would not have been able to complete it without your unwavering support and belief in both me and this project. I have learned so much from you and I am eternally grateful—as was my mother. I hope this book does you proud.

My dear partner, Michael Younan: your encouragement, love and support is integral to both this book's completion and all else that I do. I do not take for granted how blessed I am to have a partner who enables me to thrive—thank you. And thank you to your beautiful family—my family now—for taking me into their fold from the very first day and giving me so much love and support.

Finally, my late family, whose love taught me more than I ever realised. My brother, Jared, modelled courage, curiosity and the importance of living your values. These traits were learned from our mother, Lorraine, who instilled in both Jared and me a strong sense of social justice. Mum taught us, by example, that if you can do something to help, you should. I would not be the person writing this story without the sacrifices they made for me. This book is for them.

Contents

List of Tables

1

Introduction

Many young people use drugs, but few do so to the point that professional intervention is required. Why is it that some young people go "off the rails" while others seem remarkably resilient despite having faced seemingly insurmountable adversity?

In writing this book I have sought to answer a deceptively simple question: why do some young people come to experience problematic alcohol and other drug (AOD) use? The focus is on the experiences which led to drug use, rather than the use itself. The research will also question two assumptions that are quite widely held in the community. The first assumption is that drug use inevitably leads to substance abuse. The second is that young people are unable to make rational decisions about their drug use. The central argument of this book is that problematic drug use is a consequence of trauma and disadvantage that are left without support. We see in this book that this is also a classed issue: youth substance abuse is a poverty issue.

In order to investigate these issues, I undertook 61 life-history interviews with young people aged 14 to 24 who had substance abuse problems. They were recruited through two services that provide assistance to young people with drug issues across the Australian state of Victoria.

© The Author(s) 2016
K. Daley, *Youth and Substance Abuse*,
DOI 10.1007/978-3-319-33675-6_1

In doing this, I realised quickly that each young person travels their own unique pathway into problematic substance abuse. Understanding the extent of this apparent diversity is of fundamental importance for the analysis that follows. Therefore, let us begin by meeting three of the young people.

Larry, aged 20, came from a working-class family and his parents were still together. He and his two brothers had left school early and the three boys had been involved in crime. Larry had serious mental health issues and he used drugs to manage his symptoms. This was effective in suppressing his anxiety, but it inflamed his psychosis. Larry was part of a social group where masculinity was sharply defined by both machismo and aggression, and drug use was an expected social practice.

Jerry's background was quite different. Aged 19, he came from a middle-class family, and his parents had separated when he was eight, causing Jerry a great deal of emotional pain. He went to, and was expelled from, three elite grammar schools. After enrolling at the local state school, he began to thrive academically and was the dux of his graduating class. Accepted into university, he deferred for a year and travelled overseas, where his recreational drug use increased. Upon his return to Australia, Jerry abstained from all drugs, but following the death of his best friend, he became dependent upon heroin.

Lisa, 20, also had a different pathway into substance abuse. Her working-class parents separated while she was an infant and both had substance abuse issues. Lisa was raised by her mother, although this relationship was volatile. During primary school, she experienced ongoing sexual abuse, which she kept secret. In response to this secret, she began acting out, which further strained her relationship with her mother. This relationship deteriorated so badly that Lisa's mother kicked her out when she was 14. Lisa spent the next few years living on the streets, where she was "taken care of" by an older woman who introduced her to heroin. Lisa then met a young man who was so violent that Lisa ended up in intensive care.

The brief biographies of Larry, Jerry and Lisa show that these young people come from very different backgrounds: Larry came from a working-class family and his parents were still together; Jerry came from a middle-class family and his parents were separated; and Lisa was working class and her mother was a single parent. Their pathways into substance abuse were also different; Larry used drugs to manage his mental health symptoms; Jerry had been a recreational drug user before he became dependent on heroin after experiencing the loss of his best friend; Lisa was in her mid-teens when she was introduced to heroin by an older woman. Lisa was living on the street at the time. There appears to be some difference in young people's pathways into substance abuse. This diversity raises some dilemmas for policymakers: if there is little commonality in the pathways of these young people, how do we design programmes focusing on prevention and early intervention? How do we identify which young people should be included in those programmes if we have little idea of who is at risk? In order to think about these questions, we need to have a sound understanding of the reasons why some young people experience substance abuse when most do not. While at first glance it appears there is diversity among young people with drug problems, in this book I argue that it is their similarities that tell their stories.

This chapter covers four issues. First, I define what I mean by "problematic substance use". Then, I review the Australian and UK evidence on youth drug use and outline the "normalisation" thesis. After that, I look at the data on young people using AOD services. Following this, I review three explanations for problematic substance use, and then I outline the theoretical framework that underpins this book and explain the method employed to answer the research question.

Defining "Problematic Use"

It is difficult to define "problematic drug use" because whether or not drug use is "problematic" does not just depend on the quantity imbibed or injected, but it is also mediated by social context. To illustrate this point, let us suppose that two 35-year-old males use exactly the same amount of alcohol and cannabis every day. However, one has a professional occupation and lives in his own home, whereas the other is unemployed and lives in emergency accommodation. Our professional man may well view his drug use as non-problematic, whereas our homeless man is far more likely to be involved with drug treatment services. Whether drug use is problematic or not is always mediated by social context, along with individual factors both biologically (body size) and psychologically. Psychiatrist Norman Zinberg's (1984) classic work into substance use was one of the first to demonstrate that the effects of substance use are influenced by more than biochemistry alone. Zinberg (1984) proposed that the pharmacological properties were one part of what explained the impact of a substance, but a person's mindset and social setting were also significant factors. This helps us to understand why people in hospital can be on high doses of opiates for a period of time long enough to become physically dependent and yet be able to cease opiate use immediately without problem—the pharmacology of morphine is much the same as heroin; however, for a hospitalised person who is on morphine, the mindset and social setting are very different to those of persons using heroin. This is not to suggest that all heroin use inevitably leads to substance abuse or dependence. Some may use heroin recreationally, while other may develop significant dependence upon the drug.

Valentine and Fraser (2008) have argued that the distinction between problematic and recreational drug use is not a particularly useful way of categorising drug use. This is because it creates a binary which does not acknowledge the progressive continuum which drug use behaviours fall within. These authors argue that drug users are typically presented as either hedonistic pleasure-seekers (who are usually socially privileged) or poverty-stricken problematic users taking drugs for their pain-killing properties. Valentine and Fraser (2008) argue that these are inaccurate stereotypes that do not capture the diversity of human experience.

Simpson (2003) found that "dependent" and "recreational" were too discrete a category, failing to account for a group whose substance use may be problematic, but the substance being used would often change; hence, they were not dependent on a substance specifically. A third category of "persistent use" was used in his study.

Jay (1999) suggests that there are, in fact, two groups of drug users. While not mutually exclusive, he purports that their motivations are different. Firstly, he explains that the large majority of drug users are pleasure-seeking, and this is made obvious by the fact that only drugs with pleasurable effects are used excessively. The second group of drug users are those whose use is problematic. Jay (1999) argues that this group needs to be considered in context. He explains that as problematic users are only a small minority of the drug-using population, the question that should be asked is: "why do they use drugs in large quantities?" Jay contends that those who are "problematic drug users" are seeking to escape from intolerable emotional situations, whereas recreational drug users use drugs for pleasure and to increase sensory awareness. As this book unfolds, it will become clear that this is an important insight.

While I agree that there is no clear line that demarcates one group from the other, I do think that a distinction is useful to enable some sort of categorisation. Such a pragmatic approach perhaps stems from my work in services and policy areas where a problem needs to be identified in order for a solution to be developed. Not surprisingly, it is not helpful to explain to a young person asking for help that his or her substance use may not be a "problem", because the meaning of "problematic use" is constructed and everything is relative.

Among young people, the distinction between "recreational" and "problematic" use is often stark. While many young people experiment with drugs, problematic use is rare. However, those young people who do experience problems with substance abuse often have serious issues. Thus, I am reticent to accept that the term "problematic substance use" is meaningless. The category of "persistent use" is helpful here, as many of the young people in this study shifted drug use preference in response to availability. They were often not dependent on a specific substance so much as they were dependent on being substance-affected. But with all categories, there is the difficulty of developing specific definition. While any definition may be imperfect in its application, we should not forget that some young people need intensive support to assist them when they are in the grip of substance abuse, and theorising or debating whether their pattern of use fulfils the definition of a particular category would do little to assist them. Given that not all dependent use is problematic and that not all problematic use is dependent, I came to refer to these young people's drug-using behaviours as "substance abuse" as a broad categorical label. I see substance use and substance dependence as two ends of a continuum of drug-using behaviours. Substance abuse can happen at any point upon that continuum, but its characteristic is that it creates problems for the individual or those around him/her. "Substance abuse" is not a neutral term, but much less derogatory than "drug addiction". "Substance abuse" and "problematic use" are used interchangeably throughout the text.

While neither "problematic" nor "non-problematic" drug use is neatly defined, I needed an operational definition for research purposes. Given that all of the young people who participated in this study were engaged with drug treatment services, I took this to mean that they found their drug use problematic (and persistent or dependent). Therefore, I did not define problematic use by the amount of drugs that people consumed or the frequency with which they used them, nor did I apply some form of diagnostic-like categorisation. Instead, I worked from the premise that my participants had been engaged in problematic substance use (or "substance abuse") because they were participating in interventions offered by drug treatment service providers.

Recreational Drug Use

Before we look at explanations for problematic substance use, we need to look at the data on overall drug use in the community. First, I will discuss recreational drug use and then I will discuss the "normalisation thesis".

There are two main sources of data about the drug use patterns of young Australians. First, the National Drug Strategy Household Survey (NDSHS) is undertaken every three years by the Australian Institute of Health and Welfare. People are asked about their drug use and their attitudes towards drugs. The 2013 NDSHS (AIHW 2014) had a sample of 23,855 people aged 12 and over.

There are three significant limitations with this survey on drug use, and these need to be recognised: (1) some household members may not be confident that their individual data is confidential and thus not report accurately; (2) those who are not housed are not included in the survey; finally, (3) the sampling frame used for the study is not stratified by population size, so some states and territories are either over- or under-represented. Notwithstanding these limitations, the NDSHS is an important source of data on the epidemiological patterns of drug use in Australia as it is the only national data set available.

The second source of data is the Australian Secondary Students' Alcohol and Drug Survey (ASSAD) which provides figures on drug use prevalence among young people enrolled in Victorian secondary schools (Department of Health 2013). This study collects data on young people aged 12 to 17 enrolled in public, private and Catholic secondary schools. The most recent study had a sample of 4413 young people. As with the NDSHS study, there are some obvious limitations. Some young people may be reticent about disclosing their drug use patterns, and others may exaggerate their "worldliness" out of a sense of bravado. Most importantly, young people who are not at school when the survey is carried out are excluded, and some of those who are absent may be the more marginalised students who have higher levels of drug use.

A third source of data was also used for reference. The Crime Statistics for England and Wales (CSEW; ONS 2015) conducted face-to-face surveys (n = 33,350 in 2014) with households, exploring a range of issues, including drug use. This had shortcomings similar to those of the NDSHS, in that it does not access the homeless or institutionalised but does give some baseline data about drug use trends. As this study focused on crime, information on alcohol use (which is legal) was not collected.[1]

All three studies (NDSHS, ASSADS, CSEW) ask whether young people have ever used particular drugs ("lifetime prevalence") as well as whether they have used various drugs in the preceding four weeks ("period prevalence"). In this section I examine the lifetime prevalence data and I will come back to the period prevalence data later.

Table 1.1 presents the ASSAD data for those aged 17 years and the NDSHS data for those aged 14 to 19 and 20 to 29. The NDSHS is not disaggregated, so it is not possible to know the breakdown of prevalence into a single age. It would be reasonable to presume that the use is more prevalent among 19-year-olds than among those aged 14; thus combining the group dilutes the prevalence of use. Similarly, the UK figures are also not available as disaggregated data, and hence the different reporting range (16–24). Because of this difference, there is some variation between

---

[1] In England there is a school students' survey on alcohol and other drug use; however, this only provided data for young people up to the age of 15, which was too young for meaningful comparison. However, it is noteworthy that 74 per cent of 15-year-old pupils cited that they had tried alcohol in their lifetime (Fuller 2012).

Table 1.1 Drugs ever used by people in different age groups

	NDSHS[a]	NDSHS[a]	UK[b]	ASSAD[c]
Age	14–19 (%)	20–29 (%)	16–24 (%)	17 (%)
Alcohol	57.7	88.6	n/a	90.9
Cannabis	18.0	45.2	31.0	29.2
Ecstasy	3.9	22.1	10.2	5.6
Meth/amphetamine	2.0	13.4	6.8	5.6
Powder cocaine	2.1	13.6	10.2	2.4

[a]National Drug Strategy Household Survey (AIHW 2015)
[b]Crime Statistics for England and Wales (ONS 2015)
[c]Australian Secondary Students' Alcohol and Drug Survey 2011 (White and Bariola 2012)

the findings of the studies. Nonetheless, we can examine these trends. While there is variation, it is clear that most young people in all studies have tried alcohol; less than a third of teens have ever tried cannabis (18 per cent in the NDSHS study; 29 per cent in ASSAD; 31 per cent in the CSEW) and about 5 per cent of teens in Australia have tried the "party" drugs ecstasy, meth/amphetamine or cocaine, respectively.

However, if we look at the data for the older age groups, there is a sharp increase in the number of people who have used all of these drugs. In Australia, the number who have tried cannabis rises from less than one-third among the younger age group to 45 per cent among those aged 20 to 29; the number who have tried ecstasy rises from 5 per cent to 22 per cent; and the number who have tried meth/amphetamine or cocaine increases from 2 to 5 per cent to 13 per cent. From the available evidence, it appears that a significant minority of young people have tried illicit drugs by their late teens, and the proportion rises quite sharply among those in their twenties. While it is difficult to make international comparisons because of the different age aggregations, there does not appear to be significant differences in the use across the countries.

The "Normalisation" Thesis

The high rates of illicit drug use detailed in the last section have led many to claim that it has become normal for young people to engage in recreational drug use. The "normalisation" thesis was developed by scholars in Britain. One aim of these researchers was to overturn the prominent discourse that drug use was a pathological form of behaviour. In the early 1990s, the British scholars wrote extensively about the apparent "normalisation" of recreational drug use among young people (see Measham et al. 1994; Parker et al. 1995, 1998, 2002). Their work was thought-provoking.

They undertook a longitudinal study with more than 700 participants, tracking them from when they met them as 14-year-olds until they were 18. The study began in the early 1990s and explored drug use prevalence among young people. These researchers advanced the thesis that recreational drug use was now normal among young people in Britain. They acknowledged that there are a small minority of young people whose use does become problematic, but that this group is atypical. Parker et al. (1998) focused on six dimensions of drug use that were said to have become normalised: drug availability, drug trying, drug use, being drug-wise, future intentions and cultural accommodation of the illicit.

The normalisation thesis moved away from the older sociology of drug use that was developed in the early 1960s. Howard Becker (1963) had argued that drug use was a clandestine activity and that cannabis users had to take great risks to obtain marijuana (which was subject to significant social controls). Moreover, cannabis smokers had to engage in their recreational activity in secret, making sure that outsiders did not discover their "deviance". The major claim of the normalisation thesis was that the cultural taboo attached to illicit drug use had all but collapsed among the younger generation. Drug use was now so prevalent that people no longer felt the need to hide their activities or to even deny that they engaged in them.

Research in Australia has also examined the normalisation thesis. In a study of recreational drug use among young people frequenting bars and nightclubs, Duff (2005) found that the acceptability of drug use was increasing. Of the 379 participants, more than half had used illicit drugs and one in three had done so in the previous month. Further, the attitudes of the participants reflected a culture among these young people where recreational drug use was acceptable, and certainly not something for which one would be ostracised. The attitudes of these young nightclubbers were consistent with the main contention of the normalisation thesis. Drug use was no longer behaviour that had to be cloaked in secrecy; rather, drug use was now an accepted recreational activity in youth culture.

In the broader community, drug (although not alcohol) use was still stigmatised, and it was often assumed that drug use inevitably leads to substance abuse. The normalisation researchers were attempting to deconstruct this stigma by pointing out two things: recreational drug use is widespread among the younger generation; and that few of these young people experience drug-related harm (Parker et al. 1998). The architects of the normalisation thesis did not necessarily condone drug and alcohol use. Nonetheless, they wanted to emphasise an important factual point: drug and alcohol use does not usually lead to dependence.

The normalisation theorists did garner some support from policy-makers for their arguments; however, this was not for the reasons that they hoped. The normalisation theorists were trying to de-stigmatise recreational drug use among young people and challenge the common construction of youth leisure as inherently delinquent and often worse—deviant. More than a decade on, the normalisation pioneers reflected that,

> the underlying political thrust of normalisation was an attempt to cast young people in a more positive light, as reasonable, responsible agents making their drug-taking decisions, weighing up the costs and benefits of their actions, carefully deciding which drugs to take or avoid. (Aldridge et al. 2011, p. 217)

The focus on young people's agency in their drug use was intended to demonstrate that drug use was not an inherently reckless or ill-considered behaviour. However, it was a nuance overlooked by policymakers who did not take on the recommendation for de-penalisation of cannabis or to increase harm-reduction policies (Aldridge et al. 2011). Policymakers appeared to take the normalisation of recreational drug use as further evidence that young people need greater policing. This is a prime example of the overemphasis of agency and underemphasis of structure that MacDonald has emphasised is typical in explanations of marginalised youth (MacDonald 2006; MacDonald and Marsh 2001).

Later in this chapter I will outline criticisms of the normalisation thesis, but two of the arguments made by the normalisation theorists were well-founded and their contribution was important. First, there is no doubt that recreational drug use has increased among young people. Second, they were right to point out that most people who engage in recreational drug use do not develop a substance abuse problem. However, a *minority* of young people do develop substance abuse issues and this is the group that I am interested in. Let us have a look at what we know about them.

Young People in Alcohol and Other Drug Treatment

In 2013, Kutin et al. undertook a survey of all young people accessing treatment for drug and alcohol issues across the Australian state of Victoria (Kutin et al. 2014). It is known as the **Statewide** *Youth Needs Census* (SYNC). This was the first study of its kind in Australia and it asked workers to complete an online survey for each client who had an open "episode of care" on 6 June 2013. All 48 youth AOD services across Victoria were contacted and 36 services (75 per cent) provided information. In total, information was gathered on 1000 young people, representing 80 per cent of their current clients. The survey had a response rate of 84 per cent and covered key indicators of health, well-being and vulnerability.

Table 1.2 compares the drug use over the past four weeks of clients accessing AOD services with the drug use young people in the two general Australian surveys discussed previously. Table 1.2 shows that alcohol was the most commonly used drug by young people in the two general surveys but the findings were somewhat inconsistent: 62 per cent of respondents in the ASSAD survey had used alcohol, compared with 39 per cent in the NDSH survey. Roughly two-thirds (63 per cent) of those accessing AOD services had also used alcohol in the previous four weeks, similar to the ASSAD result for the general population. The similarities between the young people with substance abuse issues and the general population end there.

Table 1.2 Drug use during the past four weeks

Age	NDSHS[a] 14–19 (%)	NDSHS 20–29 (%)	ASSAD[b] 17 (%)	UK[c] 16–24 (%)	SYNC[d] 12–27 (%)
Cannabis	7.6	10.5	13.3	8.4	64.4
Ecstasy	0.6[e]	2.4	1.7	2.1	4.0
Meth/amphetamine	0.8[f]	2.1	2.3	0.5	34.9
Heroin	n/a	n/a	0.7	0.0	7.1
Cocaine	0.3#	1.5	1.5	1.7	n/a

n/a not available
[a]National Drug Strategy Household Survey
[b]Australian Secondary Students' Alcohol and Drug Survey
[c]Crime Statistics for England and Wales (ONS 2015)
[d]Statewide Youth Needs Census
[e]Estimate has a relative standard error of 25 per cent to 50 per cent and should be used with caution
[f]Estimate has a relative standard error greater than 50 per cent and is considered too unreliable for general use

Almost two-thirds (64 per cent) of those with substance abuse issues had used cannabis in the preceding four weeks, compared with 8 to 10 per cent of young people in the general population. One-third (35 per cent) of those with substance abuse issues had used meth/amphetamines in the preceding four weeks, compared with 2 per cent of the 20–29-year-olds and less than 1 per cent of teenagers; and another 4 per cent had used ecstasy compared with almost no teenagers in the mainstream population and only 2 per cent of those aged 20–29. No one in the general population reported using heroin in the preceding four weeks; however, 7 per cent of those accessing AOD services had.

The SYNC survey also found that many clients came from disadvantaged backgrounds and were often disconnected from both the education system and the labour force. Just over half (53 per cent) had experienced high levels of family conflict, and one-third (33 per cent) had been involved with the state care and protection system. Nearly two-thirds (62 per cent) had experienced either abuse and/or neglect at home, and 73 per cent of the young men had been involved with the criminal justice system. Young women were faring worse on other measures of vulnerability with much higher levels of sexual abuse, self-injury and injecting drug use. Finally, it was reported that 43 per cent of the young people "lacked any meaningful daily activity". This points to the fact that they were disconnected from both the education system and the labour force (Kutin et al. 2014).

These findings were consistent with the findings from the pilot study that was undertaken for this book (Daley 2008; Daley and Chamberlain 2009), as well as with the findings from a number of overseas studies (Catalano and Hawkins 1996; Kosterman et al. 2000; Kuperman et al. 2001). The pilot study adopted a mixed-methods design. Life-history interviews were undertaken with 12 young people accessing a youth AOD service and structured interviews were completed with 14 youth AOD outreach workers. The outreach workers provided demographic information about the 111 young people who were currently working with that service. That study found that family breakdown, abuse, neglect, parental substance abuse, involvement with child protection as well as homelessness were all common among these young people, and there were no significant differences between males and females.

This study was based in Australia, but its findings are not geographically unique. There is a well-established link between childhood trauma and later adolescent substance abuse. Rosenkranz et al. (2012) undertook a study of 16–24-year-olds entering treatment for substance abuse (n = 216), and among this sample, 90 per cent of the young women and 72 per cent of the young men had histories of psychological abuse. Similarly, several American studies examining children who were in foster care have shown issues of adolescent substance abuse to be vastly over-represented (Aarons et al. 2001; Keller et al. 2010; Traube et al. 2012). Despite the persistent finding that there is a correlation between state care, drug use and other indicators of social disadvantage, what the link is, and how it manifests, remains unclear.

Three Explanations for Substance Abuse

This section examines three explanations for problematic drug use, before outlining the approach that will be employed in this book. In the broader community, substance abuse is often seen as an individual failing brought on by poor choices or weakness of character (Alexander 2008). An alternate understanding is the biological-determinist view which argues that addiction is a disease of the brain over which an individual has little control. Social scientists offer a different view again, often drawing attention to a range of structural factors that increase the likelihood that a young person will develop a substance abuse problem.

Individualistic Explanations

In the broader community it is often said that substance abuse is an individual choice or that it reflects various types of character weakness (You Yen 2016). This view often seems pervasive, although it is given little attention in the scholarly literature. Alexander (2008) draws attention to this in his historical account of addiction. Alexander argues that only through a historical perspective are we able to understand the complex development of "addiction" as a cultural phenomenon:

> *The conventional wisdom depicts addiction, most fundamentally, as an individual problem. Some individuals become addicted and others do not. An individual who becomes addicted must somehow be restored to normalcy. There is an odd dualism built into this individual-centred depiction: addiction is seen either as an illness or as a moral defect or—somehow—both at once. Accordingly, addiction can be overcome by professional treatment or moral reformation of the afflicted individual, or both … the historical perspective does not deny that differences in vulnerability are built into each individual's genes, individual experience, and personal character, but it removes individual differences from the foreground of attention, because social determinants are more powerful.*
> (Alexander 2008, pp. 1–2)

The view that those who suffer the negative effects of substances do so because they choose to use drugs and therefore do not "deserve" help is simplistic. While it is true that substance use is an individual choice, it is hard to believe that individuals *choose* to experience problematic substance use. Nonetheless, this view has influenced some policymakers. In 1981, the "Just Say No" campaign driven by the then US First Lady Nancy Reagan perpetuated the view that drug abuse could be prevented if individuals were to make "better" choices. This rests on several assumptions of relative privilege:

1. That drug use has no significant purpose to an individual
2. That people have options and reasonably equal starting positions from which to make these choices
3. That structural factors are unrelated to drug-taking decisions

Of course, people make choices all the time, but we need to understand why some people make choices that lead to substance abuse whereas others do not. The individualist argument suggests we all make choices in a vacuum free of structural influence.

There is a strand in the individualist argument that explains substance abuse as a consequence of "bad character". This populist argument purports that some people have personality traits—fecklessness, laziness, slothfulness and so forth—that explain their excessive alcohol and other drug use. Substance abuse is a consequence of bad character rather than bad choices. In a sense, this argument explains everything and nothing at the same time. Question: "Why do people become drug addicts?" Answer: "Bad character." Question: "How do you know they have bad character?" Answer: "They are drug addicts."

There are problems with both versions of the individualistic argument that I have reviewed. Nonetheless, one should not dismiss the argument completely. It is important to bear in mind that people are conscious actors who always make choices about their lives, as the normalisation researchers had hoped to emphasise. This "obvious fact" about the human condition—that individuals do make choices—has to be incorporated into an adequate explanation of why some people develop substance dependence. Surprisingly, the next approach says people have no choice at all!

Biological-Determinist Explanations

The biological-determinist view argues that addiction is a disease and that "addicts" have an illness that has a physiological basis. One of the largest AOD research centres is the US National Institute on Drug Abuse (NIDA) which bases its research on the "science of addiction". The head of this centre is a psychiatrist, Nora Volkow, who argues that addiction is a disease of the brain (Volkow and Fowler 2000). This understanding of substance abuse is known as "the medical model".

The medical model of addiction is closely aligned with the 12-step model of treatment that is used in Alcoholics Anonymous and Narcotics Anonymous. This approach suggests that there are genetic determinants of addictive behaviour. Magnetic resonance imaging (MRI) has been used to show the effects of drug use on an individual's brain and also to argue that there is a process of neuro-adaptation where the brain becomes "addicted", thus overriding the individual's agency. However, the evidence is not in. While there may be differences, how these came about, whether or not they existed prior to substance abuse, what they actually mean is not certain. Simpson's (2003) concept of persistent use also cannot be explained within this model as the argument is that an individual's brain becomes dependent upon a chemical reaction, yet for those whose use is persistent and/or poly-drug users, the chemical reaction is not constant or consistent to substantiate dependence. So at best, these explanations can be considered as theories rather than scientific fact.

The biological-determinist view has difficulty explaining why problematic substance use is over-represented in groups with low socio-economic status. It also has difficulty explaining why many people report recreational drug use for many years, before the development of an addiction. Addiction theories tend to view drug misusers as "helpless addicts" who continue to consume simply because they cannot do otherwise. This approach precludes the role of agency altogether; and unless we subscribe to some theory of eugenics, it remains unanswered as to why these factors are over-represented among the poor (AIHW 2014).

Social Scientific Explanations

Historically, commentators have observed the lack of research of a sociological bent within the AOD field. Hamilton (1993), for instance, has argued that sociology is the "poor relation" in AOD research, and Zajdow (2005) suggests that this is because sociologists are "scared" of entering debates about drugs. However, there have been some significant contributions that are exceptions to this claim, particularly when including work from cognate disciplines such as anthropology and ethnography (e.g.: Adler 1985; Adler et al. 2012; Blackman 2004; Bourgois 2002; Bourgois and Schonberg 2009). Social scientists have traditionally taken the view that a variety of factors are involved in the development of problematic substance use and that there can be no single causal factor.

In the broader literature on drug use including the work from epidemiology and psychology, a number of authors have attempted to identify "risk factors" for substance abuse, as well as "protective factors" (Hawkins et al. 1992; Mason et al. 2011; Loxley et al. 2004). These authors draw attention to a number of risk factors, but I will use one example to illustrate their approach. The age of substance use initiation is said to be related to the onset of problematic drug use (Degenhardt et al. 2010; Degenhardt et al. 2000; Loxley et al. 2004; Mason et al. 2011). There is evidence that shows that statistically, young people who have problematic drug use began drug use earlier in life than their peers without drug issues. Research has also consistently shown that people with more chaotic drug use and those who are poly-drug users also commenced drug use at an earlier age (Degenhardt et al. 2000, 2010; Hawkins et al. 1992; Loxley et al. 2004; Mason et al. 2011). These statistics are used to conclude that the earlier in life that an individual tries drugs, the more likely they are to develop problematic substance use. Essentially, this approach identifies various factors that are correlated with substance abuse (such as early drug use), but it does not incorporate the role of human agency.

Most importantly, this argument does not explain something very significant: why do some people who try drugs early go on to develop a substance abuse problem, whereas others who try drugs early on do not? Several social scientists have raised this question. Hamilton (2004) points out that while drugs may precipitate problem use, drug use rarely leads to problem use. She, like MacDonald (2006) and Webster et al. (2004), found that risk factors alone do not throw much light on who is likely to go on to develop problematic substance use. These researchers found that in highly impoverished areas, there were people with the same number of risk factors without substance use issues. Hamilton (2004) argues that to best identify those most "at risk", it is more useful to measure the number of protective factors an individual has and that those with the least are those most "at risk".

Webster et al. (2004) found in their sub-sample of people with criminal and/or drug-using careers that those who desisted from crime and drug use had similar life troubles to those whose drug use and criminal activity persisted. However, it appears that while the number of risk factors was not a distinguishing variable, on reading the report at face value, those who were doing well at abstaining from drug use and crime were those who had more protective factors in their lives, though this comment comes only from reading the biographies of the selected participants presented in their report (Webster et al. 2004).

In order to understand these differences, we need more biographical information of individuals. For example, why do some young people have access to drugs at a very early age? Why do drugs appeal to some of these young people but not to others? What sort of families were these young people in where early drug use was acceptable? There is an increasing body of evidence that these young people often come from families where there has been child abuse, neglect, parental substance abuse, or the young person has been involved in the state care and protection system (Best et al. 2012; Keller et al. 2010; Kutin et al. 2014; Rosenkranz et al. 2012; YSAS 2012). In some cases, these factors precede drug use initiation. An adequate explanation of why some people develop problematic substance abuse must explicate the link between structural factors and human agency and understand not only the role of risk factors but protective factors also.

An Alternative Framework

Critics of the Normalisation Thesis

The normalisation thesis drew attention to the point that recreational drug use is now widespread among young people and that few of these young people were experiencing drug-related harm. The normalisation theorists were trying to de-stigmatise recreational drug use among young people so that policymakers could direct their attention to the smaller number of teenagers who were experiencing drug-related harm and to stop over-policing young people.

However, we saw earlier that this did not work and that perhaps it did the opposite by perpetuating the idea that young people's leisure is always a problem (Aldridge et al. 2011). The underlying belief that drug use is always problematic was never questioned. There was an implicit—and sometimes explicit—assumption that "adults" are morally superior and that it is the responsibility of "grown ups" to police young people's behaviour. In the eyes of some people, if drug use was becoming more widespread then punitive policies should be introduced to curb this dangerous trend. While the evidence suggested that drug use was increasing but that it was not necessarily a problem, the widespread uptake of the normalisation thesis led to harsher drug policies (Blackman 2004).

From its inception, Shiner and Newburn (1997) were critical of the normalisation thesis. They were concerned that the book made exaggerated claims about the number of young people who used drugs and how widely this was accepted. They pointed out that drug use is not a "normal" activity among young people although it is fair to say drug use is more socially acceptable than in previous generations. They also pointed out that some young people use neither alcohol nor illegal drugs and we cannot assume that they necessarily condone drug and alcohol use.

Shiner and Newburn's (1997) second objection was that the normalisation thesis gave insufficient attention to diversity within the youth population. They pointed out that the normalisation thesis "stresses the uniformity and apparent ubiquitousness of youthful drug use, and underplays the tensions and divisions that continue to exist within youth culture(s)" (Shiner and Newburn 1997, p. 513). They argued that there are still major class, gender, ethnic and regional differences among young people in Britain, and this makes it unlikely that young people engage in recreational drug use for the same reasons or in the same way.

One inference that had been drawn from the normalisation thesis was that young people are "much the same" but this overemphasises the homogeneity of the youth population. Most importantly, it distracts attention away from the different causes, as well as the diverse consequences, of drug use for different groups of young people. Shiner and Newburn (1997) concluded that there were no grounds for assuming that the choices that young people make about drugs are all the same; nor are the contexts in which they use drugs similar, and nor are the outcomes of drug use necessarily the same.

Shiner and Newburn (1997) were particularly concerned that the normalisation thesis had little to say about minority groups in the youth population. For example, did the thesis have the same applicability to homeless youth as it did to middle-class nightclub patrons? It seemed unlikely that these two groups engaged in drug use for similar reasons, and it seemed even more unlikely that drug use had the same consequences for them. Most importantly, the normalisation thesis did not explain why some young people experience substance abuse. These teenagers are both marginalised from mainstream society and very needy. Would government no longer feel the need to assist them? After all, isn't teenage drug use now "normal"? Shiner and Newburn's critique was also critiqued. Blackman (2004) argued that although Shiner and Newburn's argument shed light on some of the nuances of normalisation, their critique was premised on a misguided understanding of the postmodern condition and failed to see that normalisation was not about normalising drug use in the literal sense but that it was a concept "which may enable better understandings of drug consumption" (Blackman 2004, p. 144).

In the midst of the debate about the normalisation thesis, MacDonald and Marsh (2002) undertook a longitudinal study exploring youth transitions among people experiencing social exclusion. MacDonald and Marsh (2002) conducted a detailed study in an area with nine council housing estates in Teesside, in Northeast England. Their study was conducted between 1999 and 2001 and the data collection was a three-stage design. Firstly, 40 professionals who work with the young people were interviewed. This was followed by a 12-month participant observation. Finally, interviews were conducted with 88 young people aged 15 to 25 years; these participants were re-interviewed about 12 months later. There was a 60 per cent response rate at the second round of interviews.

The research undertaken by MacDonald and Marsh was designed to test the normalisation thesis, and it focused on the "socially excluded" who were the group that Shiner and Newburn were most concerned about. With regard to the normalisation thesis, MacDonald and Marsh stated that "[a]t best, our evidence would support a theory of differentiated normalisation" (MacDonald and Marsh 2002, p. 27). This was supported by a later paper by Measham and Shiner (2009) who reflected that their respective positions on normalisation—Measham was a proponent while Shiner a critic—did not allow for a sufficient understanding of young people's "situated choices".

MacDonald and Marsh (2002), whose findings had shown diversity even among young people from the same social class, explained their "differentiated normalisation" within a threefold typology. On the basis of their research, they identified three groups in the marginalised youth population in Teesside. The first group comprised young people who abstained from drug use and were critical of those who took drugs. The second was a large group of recreational drug users, and the third one was composed of young people who were engaged in problematic drug and alcohol use.

The young people who were recreational drug users (50 per cent of participants) held views that were broadly consistent with the normalisation thesis. They engaged in recreational drug use with other young people, did not feel stigmatised by their behaviour and thought that recreational drug use was "normal".

However, those young people who abstained from drug use (35 per cent of the participants) were critical of any drug-taking. They acknowledged a high prevalence of drug use in the area, but they refused to agree with the suggestion that drug use was "normal". The acceptance of this suggestion would have positioned them as "abnormal", whereas they felt morally superior for abstaining from drug use.

The final group in MacDonald and Marsh's typology consisted of young people who were engaged in problematic drug use (14 per cent of the sample). These people were self-defined, but they were usually partaking in daily use of various types of drugs and alcohol, and some were very heavily "into the scene". MacDonald and Marsh felt that a biographical approach was essential to disentangle their pathways into problematic substance use from the multiple forms of disadvantage they had experienced as they were growing up. Similarly, Shildrick and MacDonald

(2007) also articulate that a biographical conceptualisation of disadvantaged youth is crucial to understanding them. This is what informs the approach of this book. It is important to understand that not only there are correlations between poverty and drug use but also why this is the case.

A Biographical Approach

To understand youth substance abuse, we need to understand how people come to experience it. It has been almost 40 years since we have first come to question whether the scientific approach to understanding (observation) is the best way to understand the human experience (Merrill and West 2009; Oakley 1981). Understanding experiences is an inherently subjective endeavour and can only be done through biographical methods. There has been a "turn" towards biographical methods, which Merrill and West (2009) argue is a response to a history of omitting or under-valuing the human participant. My own biographical approach is guided by five propositions that will be used to shape the empirical analysis that follows.

Individuals Are Conscious Decision-Makers

It has already been pointed out that people are conscious actors who make choices about their lives. This is an "obvious fact" about the human condition and it has to be incorporated into explanations of substance dependence. We met Larry, Jerry and Lisa briefly and we saw evidence that they were making decisions about their lives. For example, Larry chose to use drugs to manage his mental health symptoms; Jerry decided to abstain from all drugs upon his return to Australia; Lisa made a conscious decision to not ever go home after she had been evicted by her mother. An adequate explanation of young people's pathways into substance abuse must take into account how young people make decisions about their lives, sometimes changing their minds and often reflecting on what has happened.

Structural Factors Are Important

The term "structural factors" is widely used in sociology to refer to those external factors that influence people's lives. They come in two main forms which are sometimes referred to as "material structures" and "non-material structures". Material structures relate to institutions, organisations or physical structures that typically have some form of material presence, such as the education system, the criminal justice system, the housing market and so forth. Non-material structures relate to belief systems that are external to the individual. So, for example, hegemonic masculinity is a non-material structure, as is patriarchy and other cultural beliefs about how people should act. One of the most important challenges in the analysis that follows is to demonstrate the link between external structures that influence people and how actors make their decisions. This is sometimes referred to as understanding the "link between structure and agency". The key analytic device that I will use to make this link is the notion of "situated choices".

People Make Situated Choices

The idea of a "situated choice" refers to the range of alternative forms of action (or possible decisions) that are available to an actor in any given situation. Shiner (2009) has suggested that young people make "situated choices" with regard to their drug use. To illustrate, I will give an example relating to youth drug use in Australia. When young people go out night-clubbing, they often want to use recreational drugs that heighten pleasure and increase sensory awareness. Since these drugs are illegal, they have to consider *inter alia*: which drugs are currently available in their area; whether any or all of those drugs are suitable party drugs (heighten pleasure, increase sensory awareness, etc.); the relative prices of different drugs; which drugs are the most pleasurable and whether one drug is safer than another. If we think about drug use in this way, then we start to understand why after cannabis, ecstasy, amphetamines and cocaine are the most commonly used illicit drugs in the UK and Australia among people under 30 (AIHW 2014; ONS 2015). These drugs have the required effect of heightening pleasure and increasing sensory awareness, and compared with illegal—and thus unregulated—substances, they are relatively safe, with risk of fatality being especially low. For instance, while ecstasy has traditionally been the illicit drug of choice after cannabis (though recently being overtaken by meth/amphetamine), only 0.7 per cent of young people who present at drug treatment services report that ecstasy is their drug of concern (AIHW 2013). Young people probably choose ecstasy rather than more harmful party drugs (such as ketamine or GHB), because ecstasy has the desired effect, is readily available, the risk of overdose is low, and it rarely leads to involvement with drug treatment services. When young people choose their drugs for a "night on the town", they are making "situated choices". Of course, there may be unforeseen consequences of taking any substances, but this is true for all decisions young people and adults make.

Young Substance Abusers Are Not a Homogeneous Group

A biographical approach has to take into account that young people who engage in problematic drug use are not a homogeneous group and that there are multiple pathways into substance abuse. We have seen that there is an increasing body of evidence which shows that young people with substance use issues often come from very disadvantaged backgrounds, with figures suggesting that more than a third (and almost half of girls) having been involved in the state care and protection system (Daley and Chamberlain 2009; Kutin et al. 2014). Nonetheless, it is wrong to conclude that all young people with a substance abuse problem come from these backgrounds. We saw earlier that Jerry came from a middle-class family and he had attended three private schools; however, he was very atypical in this study. Nonetheless, as I have pointed out, understanding the extent of diversity is of fundamental importance for the analysis that follows.

Action Is Usually Purposeful

Earlier, I explained that this book will also question the assumption that young people are unable to make rational decisions about their drug use. In my view, this claim causes more harm than it seeks to prevent, because it directs us away from recognising that most behaviour is purposeful, even when it involves young people taking extreme risks. By the end of this book I hope to have answered the question: why do young people continue to use drugs problematically when this involves breaking the law (fines and imprisonment), widespread opprobrium in the community, condemnation in the media, and rejection by one's peers? What purpose could their drug use possibly be serving? There is an answer—and it is not good news.

Method

To answer the question of how drug use becomes problematic for some young people, I had to think extensively about what research design would be most appropriate. The aim of the project was to explain problematic substance use within the context of individuals' life experiences and to achieve this I adopted a largely qualitative design. Within sociology, this is not a novel approach. However, much literature on youth drug use comes from psychology and psychiatry, where research is heavily couched in the framework of risk and protective factors and adopts quantitative approaches (Loxley et al. 2004; Hawkins et al. 1992). In order to provide a sound, detailed account of the complex interplay between agency and structure in young people's lives, life-history interviews were selected as the key method focusing on the biographical approach. Given that the population whom I was seeking to research were vulnerable in several ways—not all were 18 years of age, most were engaged in illicit activity (drug use) and many were homeless—there were a number of ethical issues to consider prior to undertaking the interviews and a discussion of these can be found elsewhere (Daley 2012, 2015).

The success of this research was dependent on being able to recruit participants. It was important to engage a wide array of young people participating in services. Gaining access to participants and successfully recruiting them do not always go hand in hand, though I was assisted by having the support of two youth alcohol and other drug service providers who offered services at over 15 sites across the state.

For two reasons, it was essential to collaborate with service providers for this research. The first was logistical: how else does one locate 60 young people with problematic substance use? But more importantly, it was imperative that young people were engaged with services as a mechanism to ensure that participants had some supports and resources in place should the research process be distressing in any way. I collaborated with the Youth Support and Advocacy Service (YSAS) and Barwon Youth Alcohol and Other Drug (AOD) Service in the Australian state of Victoria.

Engaging with YSAS was important as it is the largest youth AOD services provider in Victoria, operating many different programmes and providing services to clients across the state. YSAS was the first specialist youth AOD agency in Australia. It began operation in 1998 and pioneered the model for youth AOD work. They offer a variety of services, including outreach, residential withdrawal, residential rehabilitation, a supported housing service, day programmes, a young parents programme, forensic services, and primary health services. YSAS sees clients aged 12 to 21.

Barwon Youth is a generalist youth service in regional Victoria that offers a variety of programmes, including education and training and an AOD service. The AOD service has two programmes: outreach and a day programme. Barwon Youth sees clients aged between 15 and 25.

Prior to becoming a researcher, I had been employed in the sector as a youth outreach worker and this meant that developing these collaborations was a smooth and organic process. Often I knew, or knew of, the staff and management at the service sites which meant that getting "access" was not an obstacle: services were positive about the opportunity for research which they could not otherwise afford. As an "insider" of sorts, I was given an "access all areas" pass. Senior management at both services were comfortable for me to arrange my visits on my own rather than to supervise me or to arrange the first meeting with programme managers. There was an implicit understanding that as a former frontline worker, I would adopt the same philosophical approach to the young people as research participants as I did when they were clients: this involved adopting a non-judgmental approach and showing respect and care. There can sometimes be a chasm between researchers and service providers. It is important to bridge this chasm for collaboration to be successful. This can be both time-consuming and resource-intensive. Service providers are short of time and resources and they are usually concerned that researchers do not negatively disrupt programmes. Having a pre-existing relationship with the sector, I was often referred to as "one of us". It was assumed that we had a shared understanding of their work and their clients. Being an insider was integral to the success of the recruitment as too was the support of the frontline workers in these organisations, as it was these frontline workers who let clients know about the research, who arranged meetings between the clients and me, and who let me "hang out" in their spaces and immerse myself in the environments in which the clients were spending their time. The workers did not ask me to disclose what was shared between the client and me but were able to help the young person should they need debriefing later on. There was no passive resistance; rather, workers were active in enabling the research process.

This positive relationship was built on reciprocity. As the researcher, I needed to understand the nature of the work. At the beginning of data collection, the staff members at the first agency were still recovering following a spate of youth suicides in their region. There was a heavy sense of grief in the town and both clinicians and clients were distressed. It was inappropriate to begin an interviewing programme at that time. I suggested that I return to the site as my last service provider, two years later, which the site both agreed to and appreciated. They wanted to be involved but at a time that was appropriate.

Time was central to the research process. It was necessary to allow a long period of data collection to ensure a large and diverse sample was recruited. While it took time, like MacDonald (2008) reported, this population here was not "hard to reach".

I wanted to interview a cross section of the young people in the service, not only those who were outspoken or the usual nominee for youth participation activities. These people were certainly welcomed, but I also wanted to engage those who were typically quite shy with strangers. My strategy was to spend a lot of time near them, typically "hanging around". I regularly and consistently spent whole afternoons and evenings in day programmes, detoxes and drop-in centres. Here I got to know the regulars, but I also got to know the occasional visitors too. I actively sought to distance myself from the staff—not taking keys or spending any time in "Staff Only" areas. It was important to avoid exacerbating the already obvious power imbalance between myself and the young people and to assure them that what they told me as research participants would not be relayed to any of the workers. This project did not adopt an ethnographic design to the extent of Venkatesh (2008) or Bourgois (2002) who both immersed themselves in high-rise public housing tenements in areas throughout America for many years. Nonetheless, basic ethnographic principles were applied with the intention of making young people feel comfortable and familiar with me by being in and understanding their spaces and the practices which govern them (Hammersley 2007).

Young people sometimes asked who I was, but more often they watched who I was. In our banter and chats around the basketball court or the lounge room of a detox, they would watch my interactions with others and listen to how I spoke. Very often, young people—young men in particular—would look up in shock when I swore. This was an obvious marker that their perception of a researcher was someone who did not swear. Similarly, I seemed to build some credibility by being able to understand the colloquial terms for drugs and various other practices in which they partook. Frequently, I found myself strengthening my connection with them accidentally. On one occasion, a young woman wanted a sandwich but could not make it because she had just painted her nails. When I offered to do it for her, this small act received far more gratitude than was warranted. Likewise, asking a young man, "Have the dreams started yet?" when he told me he was at day seven of withdrawing from cannabis, was received with a look of connection. He had not realised that this symptom was normal. He found it comforting to hear that these dreams were common and that they would pass. These interactions which were casual and unplanned often led to deeper conversations and helped to develop a bond with the young person. Unintentionally, these interactions showed the young people that I cared about them, enabling me to become a welcome visitor. While "hanging out" with the young people, I was never able to become an "insider" in the true sense of the term. Separating myself from the staff was done reasonably well, yet while I developed very close relations with the young people, I was still older than them and not one of them.

As with every researcher undertaking anthropological methods, who I was shaped the nature of my relationship with participants. A working-class woman in my mid-twenties, I often found myself being asked the sort of advice one asks an older friend or big sister. Young women asked about make-up, menstrual cycles, relationships, body image and anxiety. They talked about fashion or asked my advice about love and everyday life. The young men often took some time to feel comfortable. Many masked their vulnerability with machismo. They were assertive in their use of shared space, sometimes punctuating their sentences with the word "cunt" and then apologising for swearing in front of a "lady". They were not trying to use standover tactics on me; rather, this was simply how they interacted with women. The more days I spent with them, the more I saw this fade. Typically, there would be a "moment" when I would see the bravado fall. These moments were always unplanned.

One young man mentioned in passing that he had had his first psychotic episode and had woken up in hospital, unsure of what had happened. I observed, "Gosh, that must have been scary". He paused. "Yeah, yeah it was," he uttered, seemingly surprised that he had admitted to that. It was these moments, often where I offered the young men a chance to be something other than "tough", which developed the richness in our relationships; where me being a young woman stopped being a barrier and instead I became simply an adult who cared. At the beginning of the research many people warned me that one does not get the same quality data from young men as from young women. There seemed to be an accepted belief that young men were inarticulate and inexpressive. At first meeting, this would seem to be the case. However, the more time I spent with the young men, the more opportunity I gave them to present themselves as more than simply full of testosterone and machismo. Slowly, in small interactions, the young men learned that I was interested in them when they were vulnerable as well as when they were tough. I was more impressed when they cried when they told me about violence. These nuances, what Komesaroff (2008) refers to as the "microethics", enabled the young men to express other dimensions of themselves—and they did so as articulately as the young women.

Interviews

In order to collect young people's biographies, I undertook one-on-one in-depth interviews. Some young people were interviewed on the day of meeting and others were interviewed after months of seeing me hanging around. Interviews were selected as the primary data-collection method because of their ability to develop an intimate space where an individual feels safe to share their story. Minichiello et al. (2008) describe the aim of the sociological life-history interview as being to "understand the ways in which a particular individual creates, makes sense of and interprets his or her life" (p. 125). Obvious limitations to this are that the participant's presentation of their story, and the researcher's interpretation of it, are highly subjective. However, the life-history interview is an instrument which allows the participants to present their life in a way that is meaningful to them, and guided by what shaped them, rather than by being confined to the predetermined categories of methods deemed to be more objective. Willig (2003) argues that the value of this type of research is that it does not seek to reduce human experience to "abstract statements about the nature of the world in general" (p. 51).

In the interview process, I drew on principles of narrative inquiry, encouraging participants to narrate their own biography and position themselves as an active agent in this narrative. Plummer eloquently describes narratives as "a most basic way humans have of apprehending the world" (2001, p. 185) He describes the narrative as the vehicle of communication and outlines two key approaches to narrative which informed my own approach. Telling one's story through developmental stages (childhood, adolescence, adulthood, etc.) is common, although it does limit the narrative to a linear sequence and may fail to afford appropriate weight to particular events. Acknowledging this, I also drew on what Plummer refers to as the "obstacle race narrative" where participants focus their story around specific events irrespective of the order in which they occurred. Tamboukou et al. (2012) suggest that a strict focus on collecting information chronologically may "close off information about unconscious realities" (p. 12) and thus restrict the depth of the data collected.

The interview as a method of inquiry is used so frequently that we often do not think critically about its epistemiological foundations. How can we uncritically accept that the data generated here is an accurate representation of the subject matter at hand? While I accept as true that most people typically tell the truth most of the time, there is more nuance to establishing an accurate representation that exceeds far beyond whether what people told me was "true" or "false".

It was the work of feminists before me who began to challenge the privileging of scientific influence on the interview. Texts pre-dating the 1970s instructed researchers to avoid answering questions that participants asked of them ("stick to the schedule") and to be "unbiased" (Oakley 1981). The presumption was that this would increase the comparability of findings from one participant (or "subject" as they were referred) to the next. The inherent assumption was that it was possible—if all things were controlled—for the interview to be an objective endeavour. However, such a line of thinking rests on the belief that the participant, or "subject", would be most neutral when the interviewer was as inanimate as a garden gnome.

But a warm rapport between interviewee and interviewer is no less subjective than an approach seeking to emulate a clinical spectator, as Manent suggests (1998). The interviewee will react to both warmth and the coldness: being impersonal is just as significant to the interviewee as being overly personal.

The assumption underpinning the positivist view of qualitative methods is that reducing an interviewer's participation increases the reliability of the data, but this assumes that the interviewer doing nothing is keeping the data "pure" or uncontaminated. This overlooks the fact that doing nothing is doing something. In the context of human interaction, it is absurd to suggest that a person sitting in silence does not have an impact on her audience. If I tell an interviewer something deeply personal and he or she offers no further query or compassion, then I will cease to discuss it and likely other personal things too. The absence of a personal response to a personal disclosure will teach me that this is not the type or depth of data the interviewer is seeking. The lack of response has told me that this information is insignificant, unimportant. Doing nothing hampers the depth and quality of the data created. In the current study, it was warmth that led to a richer description from participants as they sensed that I cared. Letherby et al. (2013) propose that objectivity is itself a value-laden endeavour and not useful for some qualitative work. Instead, they suggest a "theorised subjectivity" which "acknowledges that research is a subjective, power-laden, emotional, embodied experience but does not see this as a disadvantage, just as how it is" (p. 80).

Empiricist approaches to interviewing seek to diminish or overlook their very unique strength: *it is necessary* to know about who the researcher was and the relationship between interviewer and participants as it tells us more about how the data came about, giving the critical reader an understanding of not just the method but the process undertaken to generate it—and interviews are a process where data is generated rather than collected. To privilege objectivity in the context of a research interview is a fundamentally flawed endeavour. To ask someone about the views or experiences is a task that privileges the subjective. This is not to say that questions asked cannot be leading, but that the specifics of the query are a matter of good design rather than good data. To explicate: the data is not biased; the questions may be. Hence the necessity to know the method and interview schedule. To suggest that personal material be collected impersonally belies the obvious fact that humans usually disclose more depth the deeper the relationship they have with their listener.

So who was I as I went about this study? I was about 27 but looked considerably younger. My appearance in both dress and demeanour was "mainstream". My former work was as a youth alcohol and other drug worker, which some participants came to learn but I expect all had some sense of. My familiarity with their issues and their lives, my comfort in the spaces they were in and understanding of their sub-cultural language and phrases would have made it clear that the area I was researching was an area with which I already had some familiarity, though I doubt many thought I had ever experienced drug issues myself. I came from a very working-class background and had been exposed to many of the issues the young people in this study had faced: I understood the poverty/crime/drug use nexus before I had ever begun to work in it professionally. But I had not ever had any substance use issue myself, nor any involvement with crime. I understood poverty and had been raised in it, but I was no longer a part of it. I was now professionally employed and with a PhD scholarship in hand. I was not an "insider" in the true sense of the word. All of these things shaped my interactions with the participants. Our interactions were warm and personal. I was empathetic when they told me sad things and I laughed when they made jokes that were funny. I did not ever cry or get angry or make moral judgments on their behaviour—while I demonstrated emotion, I was essentially just an engaged listener.

There recent "reflexive turn" in sociological research asks the researcher not only to position themselves in the research but to also acknowledge the emotionality involved in the generation of research data (Holmes 2010). Consideration of this is relevant here as the stories that were collected in this research are harrowing. This raises three points:

1. How can we understand what it must have been to experience these things?
2. How did I, as interviewer, reconcile the emotions that arose in the research process?
3. How do I communicate these stories so as not to overwhelm you, the reader, while also not removing so much of the personal from the stories that you feel desensitised to the very real trauma that these young people experienced?

I do not have definitive answers for you. I do not know that we can fully comprehend what it must have been to experience another's life. T.S. Eliot wrote in East Coker (1943) that there is "[a]t best, only a limited value in the knowledge derived from experience". He went on to explain that to presume to understand things for having previously experienced them is false as each moment is new and therefore, "every moment is a new and shocking valuation of all we have been". Eliot's emphasis here is that while we can begin to see trends, they do not enlighten us to an individual's experience of something. To say it was typical for the women in this study to have a history of sexual abuse does not infer that these women's experience of sexual abuse was typical: the experience was always horrifying but always unique.

The next question that arises is about emotions. Blackman (2007) contends that discussion about methods rarely extends to a discussion about the nature of the emotional relations between interviewer and participant. He suggests that this is because of an academic requirement for the data to be "clean" but notes that this is changing, with positionality and recognition of the emotions in fieldwork becoming an accepted part of methodological discussions. It is very difficult to conceptualise how emotions could be separated from a study exploring life histories. Those telling their stories become emotional and those hearing have emotional responses too. But in addition to this, it was these emotions that I witnessed and that I felt that further pushed me to continue the study and to document these young people's lives and this motivation was in line with Holmes's (2010) claim that "how and why people feel committed to their concerns is a matter of emotional relations to other things and people" (p. 143). As much as I could have attempted to ignore emotions, my very motivation to keep going was not intellectual but emotional: I felt moved and obligated to share their story.

Lastly, the concern that was most difficult to balance was how to convey these stories in a way that would balance the need to articulate people's experiences but not be interjected with my own comments or assumptions about how it felt. Even writing this I am wrestling with how this could ever be satisfactorily managed. The story needed to be narrated, but as I wrote it, I tried to leave my voice quiet as the participants explain their lives. What follows will likely move you. I do not suggest how it will move you, but anticipate that these stories will be, for many, "a new and shocking valuation of all we have been" (Elliot 1943).

In total, 35 men and 26 women were interviewed and the sample loosely represented the age, gender and geographic composition of the broader population of youth in substance abuse treatment. Fieldwork was undertaken between 2010 and 2013. Almost all participants were from very working-class backgrounds and it was not uncommon for there to be intergenerational patterns of state-care involvement, substance abuse and trauma between children and their parents.

Ethics

The ethical considerations that came with this project involved more than meeting the standard guidelines and obtaining institutional approval. The study did receive formal approval from the RMIT University Human Research Ethics Committee (HREC); however, doing ethical research was more than simply "getting approved"—it was about being prepared to negotiate the inevitable ethical quandaries which arise when out "in the field".

There is no universally accepted way of being a "good" youth researcher. On the contrary, it is the mixed constellation of methods that various researchers use that creates a solid body of literature in the youth studies field. These methods, and the way they are employed, need to be ethical. Understanding how to be ethical is complex: not because it is inherently difficult to "do good", but because what is "good" is so rarely absolute. Clark and Sharf (2007) have asked: "What responsibilities do we, as qualitative researchers, have beyond the fulfilment, of approved informed consent?" (p. 413). In addition to consent, there are other generally accepted principles, such as beneficence and respect (see Ensign 2003; NHMRC, ARC and AVCC 2007). However, what actually constitutes being beneficent or respectful differs considerably. Hence, the idea of having ethics guidelines that are applied to all research falsely gives the impression that there is a single right way to being an ethical researcher (Shaw 2008). This assumption, that one way is more right than another, overlooks what makes the philosophy of ethics different from the philosophy of science: in science, a single truth is held to be more correct over all others; in ethics it is not only acceptable, but typical, for there to be multiple, equally valid actions (Komesaroff 2008).

Being ethical was not simply about caring for participants and ensuring they knew and were able to enact their rights, but it was about the recognition that enabling young people an opportunity to tell their story was giving them a place in the policymaking arena. As Grover notes:

Unless children are permitted to become active participants in the research process, as discussed, they will continue to be "vulnerable to representations that others impose on them" (see Barron, 2003: 33), just as they are in all other domains of life. ***To be in such a position is to have one's own voice silenced and one's fundamental right to be heard effectively quashed*** . (2004, p. 92, original emphasis)

Therefore, while it is necessary to give weight to protecting participants, it is equally important to protect them from the wrongs which arise from precluding their participation.

Participants were offered the option of using their own first name or to nominate a pseudonym, and surnames were not collected. I chose to offer young people the option of using their own names because I did not want to make the implicit assumption that their story was so shameful that they would not want to be identified. This gave young people options in the research process and all thought carefully about their decision. I discussed with the participants the implications of sharing their story (people might recognise their story, etc.). Information that might identify other people in their narratives was also changed to protect those people's identities. Three young women chose versions of the name "Jessica" and two young men chose versions of the name "Andrew". In the narrative that follows, "Jess", "Jessica", and "Jessie" are different people, as are "Andrew" and "Andy".

The Ethics of Telling Others' Lives

The young people in this study shared with me the most intimate parts of their lives. Some young people were practised at telling their story and others were telling it for the first time. There were ethical issues in protecting young people as they shared their stories without going so far as to preclude, and thus silence, them. In this book, I quote the young people extensively and often with little analysis or comment interspersed. This is partly because I feel that these young people spoke with more eloquence than I could offer them, but most significantly, I wanted their voices to permeate this account of their lives. Christensen and Prout (2002) have rightly articulated that "[t]he task of the social scientist is to work for the right of people to have a voice and be heard" (p. 483). It is in this spirit that, wherever possible, I aim for the young people's voices to "speak for themselves". At times, this is very confronting; however, to disassemble these stories to the point to which they are not confronting fails to accurately portray the experiences this research aims to give voice to.

Bourgois (2002) discussed his own dilemma about wanting to soften the sometimes ugly aspects of his field data drawn from the years he spent living in East Harlem undertaking an ethnography on the street-based crack trade. He decided against it for much the same reason as I did: as a researcher, our job is to report the worlds we are seeking to understand. Therefore, the darker our subject, the darker our writing. To add light where they may be none is a disservice to participants and research integrity. Attempting to soften our readers' experience privileges the reader over the participant. The researcher's duty is to tell the story, irrespective of how disconcerting it may be.

The aim of this book is to offer a biographical account of young people's pathways into substance abuse. An eclectic mix of sociological and psychological theories is used to help frame this, and thus, it is a psychosocial analysis. But my intention has not been to produce a theoretical analysis. At present, biographies of these young people have not been documented as a project of itself. Of course, they raise interesting points that lend well to theoretical analyses and future work of my own and others will doubtlessly undertake this task. But to start with a theoretical analysis—Marxist, feminist, through risk theories or otherwise—is to begin with the voices of others—academics—than achieve the aim of this project: to give voice to the young people themselves. Thus, what follows are the stories of 61 young men and women aged 15–24 attending AOD services in Victoria, Australia. Collectively their narratives shed light on young people's pathways into problematic substance use.

Conclusion

This chapter began with three cases of young people whose stories are detailed throughout the book. Then I defined what I meant by "problematic substance use". This was followed by a review of the Australian evidence on drug use and an outline of the "normalisation" thesis. After that, I looked at the data on young people using drug and alcohol services, before reviewing three explanations for problematic substance use.

None of these explanations—individualistic, biological-determinist or social scientific—dealt adequately with the fact that people are conscious actors who make choices about their lives.

I outlined the theoretical framework that will be used in this book. I referred to this as a biographical approach. It gives particular attention to the relationship between structure and agency, and the role of situated choices in people's lives. It also draws attention to the fact that young people with substance abuse issues are not a homogeneous group and it contends that most human action—including substance abuse—is purposeful. I outlined my approach in the form of five propositions. These propositions will be used to guide the empirical analysis that follows.

The book is structured largely in the temporal order of participants' lives. But we begin at the point that I first met them. In the next chapter we meet the participants "in the grip" of substance abuse before using the subsequent chapters to detail how they undertook the journey into problematic drug use. Chapter 3 focuses on their early childhood, which leads to Chap. 4, where we see how their early adolescent years were shaping. These chapters focus on describing the lives of the young people. Following this, we analyse the participants' pathways by gender. First, I examine the women's pathways into substance abuse, analysing the interplay of sexual abuse, self-injury and substance abuse. In Chap. 6, I examine the experiences of the young men, drawing on Connell's (2005) concept of hegemonic masculinity and Goffman's (1959) dramaturgical model of self to understand the young men's substance abuse. In Chap. 7, we see the young people in the study trying to rebuild their lives. Finally, Chap. 8 makes some recommendations on what good policy in this area needs to include. This is not an easy story to tell—and there is some heartache on the way.

References

Aarons, G. A., Brown, S. A., Hough, R. L., Garland, A. F., & Wood, P. A. (2001). Prevalence of adolescent substance use disorders across five sectors of care. *Journal of the American Academy of Child and Adolescent Psychiatry, 40*(4), 419–426.

Adler, P. (1985). *Wheeling and dealing: An ethnography of an upper-level drug dealing and smuggling community* (2nd ed.). New York: Columbia University Press.

Adler, P. A., Adler, P., & O'Brien, P. K. (2012). *Drugs and the American dream: An anthology*. Hoboken, NJ: Wiley-Blackwell.

Aldridge, J., Measham, F., & Williams, L. (2011). *Illegal leisure revisited: Changing patterns of alcohol and drug use in adolescents and young adults*. New York: Routledge.

Alexander, B. (2008). *The globalization of addiction: A study in poverty of the spirit*. New York: Oxford University Press.

Australian Institute of Health and Welfare (AIHW). (2013). *Alcohol and other drug treatment services in Australia 2011–12*. Drug treatment series 21. Cat. No. HSE139. Canberra: AIHW.

Australian Institute of Health and Welfare (AIHW). (2014). *National drug strategy household survey, detailed report 2013*. Drug Statistics Series number 28, Catalogue No. PHE 183. Canberra: AIHW.

Australian Institute of Health and Welfare (AIHW). (2015). Child protection Australia: 2013–14. Child Welfare series no. 61. Cat. no. CWS 52. Canberra: AIHW.

Becker, H. (1963). *Outsiders: Studies in the sociology of deviance*. New York: The Free Press.

Best, D., Wilson, A., Reed, M., Harney, A., Pahoki, S., & Kutin, J. (2012). *Youth cohort study: Young people's pathways through AOD treatment services*. Melbourne, Australia: Turning Point Alcohol and Drug Centre.

Blackman, S. (2004). *Chilling out: The cultural politics of substance consumption, youth and drug policy*. London: Open University Press.

Blackman, S. (2007). *"Hidden ethnography": Crossing emotional borders in qualitative accounts of young people's lives*. London: Sage.

Bourgois, P. (2002). *In search of respect: Selling crack in El Barrio* (2nd ed.). New York: Cambridge University Press, (e-book).

Bourgois, P., & Schonberg, J. (2009). *Righteous dopefiend*. Berkeley, CA: The University of California Press.

Catalano, R. F., & Hawkins, J. D. (1996). The social development model: A theory of anti-social behaviour. In J. D. Hawkins (Ed.), *Delinquency and crime: Current theories*. Cambridge: Cambridge University Press.

Christensen, P., & Prout, A. (2002). Working with ethical symmetry in social research with children. *Childhood, 9*(4), 477–497.

Clark, C., & Sharf, B. (2007). The dark side of truth(s): Ethical dilemmas in researching the personal. *Qualitative Inquiry, 13*(3), 399–416.

Connell, R. (2005). *Masculinities*. Cambridge: Polity Press.

Daley, K. (2008). Moving on: Young people and substance abuse. Honours thesis submitted to the school of Global Studies, Social Science and Planning. RMIT University.

Daley, K. (2012). Gathering sensitive stories: Using care theory to guide ethical decision-making in research interviews with young people. *Youth Studies Australia, 31*, 27–34.

Daley, K. (2015). The wrongs of protection: Balancing protection and participation in research with marginalised young people. *Journal of Sociology, 51*, 121–138.

Daley, K., & Chamberlain, C. (2009). Moving on: Young people and substance abuse. *Youth Studies Australia, 28*(4), 35–43.

Degenhardt, L., Coffey, C., Carlin, J. B., Swift, W., Moore, E., & Patton, G. C. (2010). Outcomes of occasional cannabis use in adolescence: 10-year follow-up study in Victoria, Australia. *The British Journal of Psychiatry, 196*, 290–295.

Degenhardt, L., Lynskey, M., & Hall, W. (2000). *Cohort trends in the initiation of drug use in Australia*. Sydney: NDARC.

Department of Health. (2013). *Victorian secondary school students' use of licit and illicit substances in 2011: Results from the 2011 Australian secondary students alcohol and drug survey*. Melbourne, Australia: State Government of Victoria.

Duff, C. (2005). Party drugs and party people: Examining the "normalization" of recreational drug use in Melbourne, Australia. *International Journal of Drug Policy, 16*, 161–170.

Eliot, T.S. (1943). East Coker. In *Four quartets*. San Diego: Harcourt.

Ensign, J. (2003). Ethical issues in qualitative health research with homeless youths. *Journal of Advanced Nursing, 43*(1), 43–50.

Fuller, E. (2012). *Smoking, drinking and drug use among young people in England in 2011*. London: NatCen Social Research with permission of the Health and Social Care Information Centre.

Goffman, E. (1959). *The presentation of self in everyday life*. New York: Anchor Books.

Grover, S. (2004). Why won't they listen to us? On giving power and voice to children participating in social research. *Childhood, 11*(1), 81–93.

Hamilton, M. (1993). Sociology: The poor relation in alcohol and drug research? *Drug and Alcohol Review, 12*(4), 359–367.

Hamilton, M. (2004). Preventing drug-related harm. In M. Hamilton, T. Kind, & A. Ritter (Eds.), *Drug use in Australia: Preventing harm*. Melbourne, Australia: Oxford University Press.

Hammersley, M. (2007). *Ethnography: Principles and practice* (3rd ed.). New York: Francis Routledge.

Hawkins, J. D., Catalano, R. F., & Miller, J. Y. (1992). Risk and protective factors for alcohol and other drug problems in adolescence and early adulthood: Implications for substance abuse prevention. *Psychological Bulletin, 112*(1), 64–105.

Holmes, M. (2010). The emotionalization of reflexivity. *Sociology, 44*(1), 139–154.

Jay, M. (1999). Why do people take drugs? *International Journal of Drug Policy, 10*, 5–7.

Keller, T. E., Blakeslee, J. E., Lemon, S. C., & Courtney, M. E. (2010). Subpopulations of older foster youths with differential risk of diagnosis for alcohol abuse or dependence. *Journal of Studies in Alcohol and Drugs, 71*(6), 819–830.

Komesaroff, P. (2008). *Experiments in love and death: Medicine, postmodernism, microethics and the body*. Melbourne: Melbourne University Press.

Kosterman, R., Hawkins, J. D., Guo, J., Catalano, R. F., & Abbott, R. D. (2000). The dynamics of alcohol and marijuana initiation: patterns and predictors of first use in adolescence. *American Journal of Public Health, 90*(3), 360–366.

Kuperman, S., Schlosser, S. S., Kramer, J. R., Buchols, K., Hesselbrock, V., Reich, T., et al. (2001). Risk domains associated with an adolescent alcohol dependence diagnosis. *Addiction, 96*(4), 629–636.

Kutin, J., Bruun, A., Mitchell, P., Daley, K., & Best, D. (2014). *Statewide youth needs census 2013 technical report: Young people in AOD services in Victoria, Victoria-wide results*. Melbourne, Australia: Youth Support + Advocacy Service.

Letherby, G., Scott, J., & Wiliams, M. (2013). *Objectivity and subjectivity in social research*. London: Sage.

Loxley, W., Toumbourou, J. W., Stockwell, T., Haines, B., Scott, K., Godfrey, C., et al. (2004). *The prevention of substance use, risk and harm in Australia: A review of the evidence*. Canberra, Australia: Australian Government Department of Health and Ageing.

MacDonald, R. (2006). Social exclusion, youth transitions and criminal careers: Five critical reflections on "risk". *Australian and New Zealand Journal of Criminology, 39*(3), 371–383.

MacDonald, R. (2008). Disconnected youth? Social exclusion, the "underclass" & economic marginality. *Social Work & Society, 6*(2), 236–248.

MacDonald, R., & Marsh, J. (2001). Disconnected youth? *Journal of Youth Studies, 4*(4), 373–391.

MacDonald, R., & Marsh, J. (2002). Crossing the Rubicon: youth transitions, poverty, drugs and social exclusion. *International Journal of Drug Policy, 13*, 27–38.

Manent, P. (1998). *City of man*. Princeton, NJ: Princeton University Press.

Mason, W. A., Toumbourou, J. W., Herrenkohl, T. I., Hempill, S. A., Catalano, R. F., & Patton, G. C. (2011). Early age alcohol use and later alcohol problems in adolescents: Individual and peer mediators in a bi-national study. *Psychological Addictive Behaviour, 25*(4), 625–633.

Measham, F., & Shiner, M. (2009). The legacy of "normalisation": The role of classical and contemporary criminological theory in understanding young people's drug use. *International Journal of Drug Policy, 20*, 502–508.

Measham, F., Newcombe, R., & Parker, H. (1994). The normalisation of recreational drug use amongst young people in north west England. *British Journal of Sociology, 45*(2), 287–312.

Merrill, B., & West, L. (2009). *Using biographical methods in social research.* London: Sage.

Minichiello, V., Aroni, R., & Hays, T. (2008). *In-depth interviewing* (3rd ed.). Sydney: Pearson Education.

National Health and Medical Research Centre, Australian Research Council & Australian Vice Chancellors' Committee. (2007). *National statement on ethical conduct in human research.* Canberra: Australian Government.

Oakley, A. (1981). Interviewing women: A contradiction in terms? In H. Roberts (Ed.), *Doing feminist research* (pp. 30–61). London: Routledge and Kegan Paul.

Office of National Statistics. (2015). *Tables for drug misuse: Findings from the 2014 to 2015 CSEW.* Retrieved March 14, 2016, from https://www.gov.uk/government/statistics/tables-for-drug-misuse-findings-from-the-2014-to-2015-csew

Parker, H., Aldridge, J., & Measham, F. (1998). *Illicit leisure: The normalization of adolescent recreational drug use.* London: Routledge.

Parker, H., Measham, F., & Aldridge, J. (1995). *Drug futures: Changing patterns of drug use amongst English youth.* London: Institute for the Study of Drug Dependence.

Parker, H., Williams, L., & Aldridge, J. (2002). The normalization of "sensible" recreational drug use. *Sociology, 36*(4), 941–964.

Plummer, K. (2001). *Documents of life 2: An invitation to critical humanism.* London: Sage.

Rosenkranz, S. R., Muller, R. T., & Henderson, J. L. (2012). Psychological maltreatment in relation to substance use problem severity among youth. *Child Abuse and Neglect, 36*(5), 438–448.

Shaw, I. (2008). Ethics and the practice of qualitative research. *Qualitative Social Work, 7*(4), 400–414.

Shildrick, T., & MacDonald, R. (2007). Biographies of exclusion: Poor work and poor transitions. *International Journal of Lifelong Education, 26*(5), 589–604.

Shiner, M. (2009). *Drug use and social change: The distortion of history.* Basingstoke, UK: Palgrave Macmillan.

Shiner, M., & Newburn, T. (1997). Definitely, maybe not: The normalisation of recreational drug use amongst young people. *Sociology, 31*(3), 511–529.

Simpson, M. (2003). The relationship between drug use and crime: A puzzle inside an enigma. *International Journal of Drug Policy, 14*(4), 307–319.

Tamboukou, M., Andrews, M., & Swuire, C. (2012). Introduction: What is narrative research? In M. Andrews, C. Squire, & M. Tamboukou (Eds.), *Doing narrative research* (2nd ed.). London: Sage.

Traube, D. E., James, S., Zhang, J. J., & Landsverk, J. (2012). A national study of risk and protective factors for substance use among youth in the child welfare system. *Addictive Behaviours, 37*(5), 641–650.

Valentine, K., & Fraser, S. (2008). Trauma, damage and pleasure: Rethinking problematic drug use. *International Journal of Drug Policy, 19*, 410–416.

Venkatesh, S. (2008). *Gang leader for a day: A rogue sociologist takes to the streets.* London: Penguin.

Volkow, N. D., & Fowler, J. S. (2000). Addiction, a disease of compulsion and drive: Involvement of the orbitofrontal cortex. *Cerebral Cortex, 10*(3), 318–325.

Webster, C., Simpson, D., MacDonald, R., Abbas, A., Cieslik, M. A., Shildrick, T., et al. (2004). *Poor transitions: Young adults and social exclusion.* Bristol, UK: The Policy Press.

White, V., & Bariola, E. (2012). *Australian secondary school students' use of tobacco, alcohol, and over-the-counter and illicit substances in 2011.* Drug strategy branch, Australian Government Department of Health and Ageing: Victoria, Australia.

Willig, C. L. (2003). *Introducing qualitative research in psychology: Adventures in theory and method.* Great Britain: Open University Press.

You Yenn, T. (2016, March 10). Why low-income parents may make "poor choices". *The Straits Times.* Retrieved March 11, 2016, from http://www.straitstimes.com/opinion/why-low-income-parents-may-make-poor-choices

Youth Support + Advocacy Service (YSAS). (2012). *YSAS snapshot: Findings from the YSAS client census October 2012.* Melbourne, Australia: Youth Support + Advocacy Service.

Zajdow, G. (2005). What are we scared of? The absence of sociology in current debates about drug treatments and policies. *Journal of Sociology, 41*(2), 185–199.

Zinberg, N. (1984). *Drug, set and setting: The basis for controlled intoxicant use.* New Haven, CT: Yale University Press.

2

Dancing with Death

Problematic substance use is often seen as a sign of adolescent delinquency. Some young people accessing youth drug treatment services fit the common perception of what a "drug user" looks like, but most just resemble ordinary teenagers. As I began spending time with these young people, there seemed to be many explanations for why they had developed substance abuse issues. Many told me that they had fallen in with the "wrong crowd"; others explained that they had "always been naughty". Some used drugs as a way of managing mental health symptoms. Many of the women and two gay men explained that drug use was something they did with their boyfriends. Some took a long time before they saw use as a problem because it was something they had always done with their parents. Each of these explanations made some sense, but there seemed to be a lot of diversity—perhaps the explanation of these things being "a bit of bad luck" had more traction than I had assumed.

There is little research exploring just *who* constitute the population of young people accessing treatment in Australia. Until 2013, there had been no comprehensive statistical information on the number of young people in treatment. Victoria is the only state which has a statewide service system, but there are many separate service providers each with their

© The Author(s) 2016
K. Daley, *Youth and Substance Abuse,*
DOI 10.1007/978-3-319-33675-6_2

own unique record-keeping processes. There is minimum data required for those in receipt of government funding (AIHW 2013); however, this lacks any detail, and to further complicate matters, it reports on the number of treatment episodes rather than the number of individuals. Thus, individuals receiving intensive supports tally up many episodes compared with a young person on a diversionary order who may have one treatment episode. Therefore, it is not possible to make inferences about the population as the figures over-represent some and under-represent others. The two groups are likely to have different needs.

In the 2013 Statewide Youth Needs Census (SYNC: Kutin et al. 2014) of young people accessing drug treatment services in Victoria, it was found that 46 per cent of young people were disconnected from school and half of them (51 per cent) had been suspended or expelled, indicating that many were seriously disadvantaged in the labour market. Disconnection from family was very high, with 41 per cent of young women and 28 per cent of young men separated from family, indicating that many had experienced serious family trauma (Kutin et al. 2014; Daley and Kutin 2013).

Although these statistics do not illuminate whether these issues precipitated or followed substance abuse, some factors were almost certainly apparent from very early in life, prior to any drug use. These figures show that there are clear trends which mark young people in treatment as "different" from other young people of the same age. This diminishes the veracity of the "bad luck" explanation. Therefore, it was necessary to search more deeply to understand the pattern among the seemingly disparate explanations offered in the cursory discussions I was having with young people in the current study.

This chapter focuses on how these young people described their lives prior to entering AOD treatment services. First, it draws attention to the dramatic events and extreme risk-taking that characterised these young people's lives. Second, I note that young people are always conscious actors making decisions about their lives even in the most extreme circumstances. I refer to these decisions as "situated choices" because they were often constrained by external factors over which the young person had little control. Finally, the chapter uncovers why these young people continued using drugs even when they were putting their lives at risk.

Extreme Risk-taking

It took little time to realise that these young people's lives were characterised by dramatic events. Amber, 17, was six months' pregnant when I met her. She had no family support and no savings. She had been searching for accommodation, but without a job she had little chance of success. Andreas wanted to look for work or return to school, but he was due for sentencing in a month's time and faced the prospect of incarceration. Damian was in treatment for posttraumatic stress disorder after being seriously assaulted by a policeman. Each young person seemed to be in the midst of a significant event or episode. Many of these things seemed traumatic enough to explain their heavy drug use; however, some things did not add up. For instance, while these events seemed significant to an outsider, the young people themselves spoke about them very matter-of-factly. The way they spoke about these events was so inane and ordinary that it seemed as though these events *were* in fact inane and ordinary.

In lay discussions about young people and substance abuse, turns of phrase such as "teenage rebellion" and "fallen off the rails" litter the conversation. These all focus on the drug use being an entirely individual decision made in a vacuum free of structural influences. While this explanation is simplistic, there were some cases where it appeared to have credence. For some participants, mostly the men, "reckless" or "risky" behaviours could be seen in their drug-use patterns. Jake had been experimenting a little with alcohol and other drugs, but it was his entry into the subcultural world or graffiti artists which saw this escalate:

> I dabbled with a few things, but I wasn't into them. I was hanging out with the older boys, the graffers and that. I did all sorts of stuff with them—speed, heroin … just whatever was going. I did my first pill with them.

Jake's case shows that the drug use was not always as desirable as the social bonding with which it was tied. For other young people, drug use was desired, though again, there were decision-making processes at play in the choice of drugs being used.

Jahl encountered many high-risk situations. Living on the streets from a very young age, as well as being small in stature, meant that he was particularly vulnerable to falling victim of the predatory behaviour of others. In the early hours of the morning on one of his nights on the street he was approached by a man who offered him a cigarette. After talking a while the man persuaded Jahl to steal some items from a shop in exchange for some cash. Jahl went to the supermarket with the man to do this. After leaving the supermarket the man introduced Jahl to another man:

> *This guy is fresh out of prison—tattoos and stuff—he was a bad cunt. Anyway, we started talking to him, and we ended up going off to Richmond where he scored heroin. I was like, "What the fuck?!", and the next thing I know he's got me to go and buy his needle and he's sitting there whacking up and shit. I am 13 years old.*

Shortly after, the man then offered Jahl some cannabis in a peace pipe:

> *The choof had white all the way through it—white bits—and I thought it looked like really good choof. I wouldn't have taken it if I'd known it was laced. I started smoking it, but then half an hour later I am freaking out on the floor, I am out of my brain. I don't remember the whole day from then on. The first guy had left so it was just me and the guy out of prison. It was just me and him on our own ... he takes me back to these flats and I just woke up and there was this guy spooning me on this mattress in the lounge room and I was like, "What the fuck?!", but I couldn't move. I actually couldn't move. When I woke up, he dropped me off at the corner of his street and I am waking up from the worst feeling in my whole life. Two days later I look at my arm and he'd fucking injected heroin into me. There were two dots on my arm and it was all bruised up and shit. That's a big thing that I am going to carry with me.*

Jahl's experience shows that despite very limited options, he was actively making decisions. While he welcomed the cannabis, he did not want to use it if it was laced with other substances. He was also scarred by his experience of being given heroin and the lack of memory about what had happened afterward. Jahl made other situated choices. He made the decision to steal as it would provide him with much needed money. This decision was not desirable but the best of very limited options. However,

Jahl was less active in regard to his personal safety. While he felt safe in the company of the first man, it seems as though he was immediately uneasy in the company of the second. Despite this, he remained with him. It is unknown whether he did not trust his instincts or whether the need to raise money was so high that he was forced to compromise his own safety—possibly a combination of both. When I asked if he had been tested for blood-borne viruses as a result of this encounter, Jahl said that he was too scared to know the results.

The combination of vulnerability and limited choices was something that was very prevalent among the women. When Katte was living on the streets, she was "taken care of" by some of the older people. At 14 she was the passenger in the front seat of a car driven by a man in his twenties who was loosely acquainted with someone in Katte's group. He indicated that he was going to buy alcohol for them:

> We went past so many bottle shops and I was like, "Um, what are we doing? There's a bottle-o just there?", and he's like, "Yeah, I am going to a really good one". Then he pulls over to this place and he just smoked some peace pipes. I was really creeped out … then he was being sleazy and he kept trying to kiss me and shit, and I was like, "Fuck off", and I was pushing him off of me and I just kept trying and trying. He hit me and shit, and was like, "You're a fucking little bitch", and I was just bawling my eyes out … Then he started to drive off again, and I jumped out of the car. I didn't care if I had a huge scar up my arm, I was just like, "I am not staying here with him, I'll get raped" … so I jumped out of the car while it was moving.

Here we see Katte quite literally make the decision to place herself in harm's way to avoid being raped.

Being on the streets was not the only source of danger. Stevie was staying with her girlfriend Tash and Tash's child in high-rise public housing. One day Stevie was raped by a man who lived in the building. She was too scared to report the incident in case he got angry and returned to their flat when Tash and the child were home. Stevie was deciding between reporting her rape and keeping her family safe. Stevie, like Katte and Jahl, was in circumstances where the options were bleak; nonetheless, we see each of them actively reasoning and rationalising their behaviours. These young people were active agents making decisions but with options that were deeply problematic. Stories like these pervaded participants' narratives, as did experiences of accidental overdoses—both of which were discussed as accepted parts of the worlds in which participants lived.

Overdosing is something closely associated with heroin, although to some extent that is a mistruth. Almost all fatal overdoses are a combination of combined drug toxicity where benzodiazepines—such as Xanax or Valium—are in the body system and then a short-acting central nervous system depressant—heroin or alcohol—is used as well (Dwyer 2013). Benzodiazepine effects increase in intensity over time, whereas a drug like heroin works almost immediately. Having the former in the body prior to using heroin or alcohol can see the effects of the two drugs peak simultaneously and the nervous system being depressed to the extent that breathing stops. The "on the nod" effect opiate users seek can walk a close line with fatal overdose. Thus, most fatal overdoses happen when one is using alone and nobody is able to administer the opiate antagonist drug, Naloxone (also referred to as "Narcan"). Naloxone, which is administered by ambulance officers, pauses the effects of opiates on the brains receptors which gives the body time to process the drug and reduce its level in the blood.

Ben had overdosed twice. Both times he was with friends, who gave him mouth-to-mouth to keep him breathing until the ambulance arrived and administered the injection of Naloxone. Similarly, Jerry had had several overdoses. The frequency at which young people had had more than one near miss with death suggested, at face value, that they were either suicidal or unable to learn from their mistakes. It made little sense that the benefits of the drug could be so great that one near-death was not a sufficient learning curve. I inquired further.

Jerry's most recent overdose had left the previously athletic young man with permanent injury. The first overdose was at a friend's house, where the friend's mother performed mouth-to-mouth. His parents were notified, and given they were unaware of Jerry's heroin use, I queried how they reacted: "I think they were just really worried at that point. They weren't angry, just worried."

Jerry's next overdose came when he was travelling overseas with a couple of friends:

My plan wasn't to go there and use, I just got so shitfaced … I don't remember anything … Then I got airlifted to Thailand … I had an 80 per cent chance of dying, my kidneys failed, my lung was punctured.

Jerry was in hospital for three months before he was able to fly home to Australia. He was transferred straight to a private hospital in Melbourne with the aid of a family member who was a doctor there. He stayed there for six weeks, which meant that after the overdose, he had accumulated more than four months' abstinence. Spending weeks laying in a ward, his depression worsened. This combined with the grief of a friend's death earlier in the year led Jerry to relapse soon after he was released from hospital.

Ebony had had several accidental heroin overdoses, although her explanation that, "When I've woken up I didn't give a shit if I died" suggests a degree of suicidality that may have contributed to her frequently high-risk drug-use practices.

Ally and her boyfriend had a daily heroin habit. She overdosed at his house:

His grandma walked in and I was blue. He thought I was joking and then I started fitting and fell out of bed. They called the ambos … then the cops came because I had died. They were going to charge him with attempted manslaughter … [his grandmother] went to my parents and told them … they went crazy.

For Ally, this experience was a wake-up call. Although she ran away from her parents who had tried to "ground" her, she called her worker immediately to get a place in detox. For others, overdosing was part of the drug-using life. Andreas's discussion about it illustrated this well:

Recently we were at this guy's house, and this girl had 50 bricks in an hour, and she'd drunk a bottle of methadone as well and we woke up and she was dead. Yeah, she died … [she was] 15 or 16. So that was pretty bad. And another person died about a year ago, one of my mates. Overdosed on Xannies and then choked on his vomit. That's happened to me a couple of times—where my mates have had to move my tongue around 'cause I take too many and pass out after a drink.

Andreas's story can be explained in an individualist explanation as foolish: he had seen first-hand the lethality of drug use yet persisted with using them. But this happened to many participants, and it was clear that they were not fools. The question at hand seemed to be not why they were so foolish but what benefit were they receiving from the drug that outweighed the risk of death?

Not only was there a risk of overdose, but many participated in activities they did not like in order to procure their drug of choice. For some, an accepted way of raising money was sex work. Most of the participants who engaged in sex work had been homeless but were below the minimum eligible age for government financial assistance. Government policy stipulates that children under the age of 17 must be enrolled at school and children under the age of 18 without a caregiver should receive state intervention. The practice is much different. Policing young people who are not at school is largely the responsibility of the parents. For young people who had no parent or other caregiver, or whose parent or caregiver does not enforce school attendance, the notion of "compulsory" schooling is foreign. For young people who are without a caregiver, school is a near impossible task: an absence of secure accommodation makes attending school infeasible. While these young people should, technically, be able to receive access to Out of Home Care, the under-resourced system has no mechanism in place to sufficiently identify these young people, and when they do come to the attention of the relevant authorities, there are often few, if any, placement options available. The care system prioritises infants due to the risk of death being far greater were they to stay in unsafe environments. A combination of these factors places teenagers in very vulnerable positions.

Ineligibility for government assistance is premised on the belief that young people are in the care of either a parent or the state; this renders the homeless teenager with few options to raise money. Jai's first year of homelessness was financed through sex work while he was unable to access financial assistance from Centrelink. His entry into sex work was accidental. Having recently "come out", he was seeking to meet other gay teens, so he entered the online world:

> *I found a gay chat room online and started chatting. Then I got offered money for, yeah, in exchange for that … I thought, "Wow, that'd be great" … I didn't realise at the time what the ramifications would be; what I would have to do. … [then] I did my first job. It was kind of, interesting. I met really, really disgusting guys.*

Jai moved on to street-based sex work briefly, but he found this both unsafe and degrading and soon moved into the world of escorting. This was not something he enjoyed, but despite this, Jai's homelessness created desperation for both accommodation and money. Ineligible for government assistance because of his young age, sex work was a way of satiating this desperation:

> *I never had to sleep on the streets. I've always just, well, it's the perks of being gay and homeless—it makes life a bit easier. Being able to sleep around and kind of go from one guy's house to the next, or to be doing jobs escorting, … well, making the best of a bad thing happening really.*

When I asked Jai if the drugs helped him, Jai explained that they helped him "deal with it—yep, totally". Jai's sentiment that being a young gay man was a "perk" was similar to some of the young women who felt that they were taking advantage of their gender when trading sex for money, drugs, safety or accommodation. These participants seemed to accept that as a young female they were not entitled to gender equity. Roxanne expressed remorse about using her gender to get access to drugs:

> *I never did sex or anything for drugs, but I made boys think that I would and took their drugs … It's kind of easy for a girl to get drugs, and especially heroin, because not many girls who do it are single … and all male users really want is heroin and a girl to use with, so it makes it pretty easy if you are a girl and want to get drugs.*

In statements such as these we begin to see gender as a factor in young people's pathways into substance use. The practice of drug use was a gendered experience: when a man and woman were to use drugs together, there was often a power hierarchy. In Roxanne's reflection above, she felt that she took advantage of her "femaleness" to obtain drugs. However, it is probable that the dealer himself felt that he was using his power as drug dealer to obtain Roxanne's company. It is left unquestioned by Roxanne that the dealer would be a man. It is likely the dealer felt that having the drugs which Roxanne was dependent upon gave him power to obtain the company of a young woman who would not otherwise be interested in him.

Gender roles like this were common. Voni expressed a similar sentiment when explaining how she financed her habit, "Anyway I could. You know, just … I was going out with dealers. Just the usual; what girls can do." Her case was typical of others who participated in an informal type of sex work, sometimes referred to as 'survival sex'. The woman engages in an undesirable sexual relationship with a man in exchange for accommodation, drugs and/or money.

Ebony's explanation of her "decision" to enter into sex work was frequently couched in explanations that it was the only acceptable form of crime and that acquisitive crime was simply not comprehensible to her as she identified strongly as a Christian. Ebony's "choice" was to sell herself over stealing from another. Certainly, two undesirable choices, but we can see that even in such dire circumstances, Ebony was using agency to negotiate her options yet it seemed that an ingrained truth for these young women was that the female body was a commodity.

Jessy has been street sex-working for some time. For Jessy, and for most of the young people who participated in sex work, her drug use escalated as a result of needing to be high to be able to block out the reality of these evenings on the street. Increased use meant an increased tolerance, which meant that more drugs were needed to get the same effect. In turn, her nights working went from one week to daily at a rapid rate. At an equally rapid rate, Jessy's drug problem flourished. Despite the increased income which came with sex work, it appeared to be accompanied by an even greater increase of life complexity. Despite many engaging in sex work to increase their ability to finance their habit, their habit increased concurrently which rendered the young people far worse off, as the more expensive their drug habit was, the less feasible it was for them to leave the sex industry.

It is clear that there were significant issues in the lives of the young people. The risks they had taken were not because they were too young to think properly—their ability to enact reflective thought in other areas of their lives made clear that these young people were conscious actors. I sought to understand the structures in which they were so bound that the options from which they were choosing were so dire. Given that illicit sex work had not reduced young people's drug use and that drugs were clearly not being used for recreational partying, I reasoned that their use persisted because the unseen positive effects outweighed the very apparent negative effects. So I asked each of the participants what they liked about using drugs.

"Drugs Make You Feel Better"

Young people's answers to what they liked about using drugs were remarkably similar and there was no difference between women and men. Most could explain the function of their drug use easily and in a single sentence. Ben, for instance, stated clearly: "It took the thoughts away from my head." James's explanation was almost identical: "To stop thinking about things." Similarly, Stacey explained why she liked being stoned: "I didn't feel anything. I didn't worry about stuff." There was a common theme that was very clear, but less clear was why so many young people would want to stop feeling. Brandon was more elaborate in just why he liked being able to stop his thoughts:

> I think about the bad things a lot. It doesn't get out of my mind, no matter what I do, so I use drugs to make me feel better about myself, to make me feel differently. That's why I kept smoking a lot—it gave me something to do, put the shit out of my life.

Several participants, all of whom had a mental health diagnosis of either attention deficit hyperactivity disorder or obsessive compulsive disorder, both of which present with considerable mania and racing of thoughts, used drugs to slow this down. Maddison explained:

> *The main thing I liked was that it helped with my attention—I wasn't all muddled in my thoughts and mainly it helped me make up my mind. My thoughts were at a normal pace—not racing.*

Maggie, whose anxiety prevented her sleep, also liked the effects of drugs which depressed the central nervous system:

> *It relaxes me, it slows me down. It slowed all my thought processes down. It puts things in order in my head and it clarifies a whole lot of things so that I can just see one thing at a time.*

The discovery of a drug which slowed down a permanently racing mind was very welcome for those who had been feeling muddled.

Drugs which depressed, rather than stimulated, the central nervous system were by far the preference for all of the young people in this study. While reference to young people and drug use often focuses on "party drugs" taken in clubs and at parties, ecstasy and amphetamines were not often used among this cohort. Depressants numb people's central nervous system, reducing both physical and emotional feeling as well as sensory and cognitive capacity. This is not to suggest that depressants are more likely to lead to a problem because they are intrinsically worse but that the pharmacological effects of depressants are more appealing to those seeking to pause their thoughts and feelings. Stimulants do the opposite—increase the body's senses making one hyper-aware of how one feels. Matt's short and sharp reply to what he liked about drugs—"It numbed me … I didn't have to think about shit"—indicated the difference between the young people in this study and young drug users more generally. Where general youth drug use is central to socialising and increasing sensory responses to create higher states of awareness, the young people in this study wanted the opposite. Mary said poignantly: "I always did drugs to avoid reality rather than enhance reality." Desperate to avoid and escape their realities, there was a natural magnetism between these young people and depressant drugs. Amy elaborated on the function of her drug use:

It just numbed everything; I just wanted to forget about life. It just made you feel good—like you were actually somebody.

I asked Amy when the feeling of not being somebody began, and she explained:

It probably started when I was a kid—from family violence, and no one knew about anything—feeling that no one cared.

These feelings of abandonment and not being cared for were similar to the sentiments shared by Jai, whose parents had died and whose grandparents abandoned him when he revealed that he was gay. He offered a detailed insight into why feeling numb was so desirable:

It's the trauma. It's being discarded as just a piece of lint pretty much. Just being belittled and going and doing drugs to become a bigger person and to deal with people in my life ... [drugs were a] confidence builder and helped to deal with people who were really quite scary and that's the only way to get respected in the group—to do drugs.

Abandonment and a lack of family support gave some insight into why these young people wanted to stop their thoughts and feelings. Homes which lacked care and safety were increasingly becoming a common theme.

Jessica's inner turmoil was inescapable and its source was the family violence she lived with. Using drugs with her mother became a salve: "You don't have to feel the way you feel, you can just have a bong and pretend that things are different when they're not. It's an escape."

Not all the participants used drugs as pain relief. Jerry, the young man who overdosed in South-east Asia, had tried a variety of drugs with his friends during adolescence. He was typically smoking cannabis and taking ecstasy through the week and then would use "harder" drugs on the weekend. He used ice for a while, mostly smoking it. "I injected it a few times, but I never really got into it." But then heroin came into the scene, which had much greater appeal to Jerry, although it was a very occasional thing. It was after Jerry finished high school that heroin became a real issue for him. When I asked the appeal of heroin, Jerry was reluctant to suggest it was self-medication and this seemed closely tied to ideas of autonomy. He seemed embarrassed that he was struggling with his emotions despite the event that precipitated his depression being deeply shocking:

> I don't like to blame it on things 'cause it's just me, really … [but] when my best mate died, I just felt like all I wanted to do was be numb, pretty much.

Similarly, for Shawn heroin was also a way of managing grief:

> It just made you numb to everything—I didn't feel pain. I remember when my stepmum's mum died and I'd been clean for eight months, and I used smack, because I knew [it would stop the pain] … it blocks everything out and you can just forget. Make it like it didn't happen for a couple of hours.

Despite there being an emotional need for substance use to sedate psychological turmoil, many of the young people were still making "situated choices" about their drug use. As outlined in Chap. 1, the presentation of young drug users as simply hedonistic pleasure-seekers unable to make reasoned decisions and reckless in their behaviours overlooks the options that youth are faced with. Shiner and Newburn (1997) accurately point out that young people are not homogenous and that their reasons for substance use are diverse. They are also agents able to make decisions about their drug use; it is not simply that they seek out any drug in any amount and in any combination. The common representation of young people is that they lack adequate cognitive capacity to negotiate decisions and this assumption dangerously overlooks the contexts of young people's drug-using choices. Research into other areas demonstrate that even in serious situations such as war, young people are able to negotiate decisions about safety and risk (Newman 2005). To suggest that youthful drug use is a consequence of poor decision-making is a neat way to overlook such questions as "Why does a young person want to use substances that numb their thoughts and feelings?" or "What environments are young people in where drugs are available and appropriate way to deal with emotional pain?"

The youngest participant, Jahl, whose primary drug was cannabis, explained his own negotiations with various drugs:

I was getting into shard [methamphetamine]. When I came out of juvie [youth detention] I tried it once and I liked it. Then every time I got the money up, I'd go and get it. It's really expensive, it's like a treat. I'd go and have a little bit, and then go and have another little bit, and before I knew it, I was liking it too much. It was getting hectic, so I was like, "No more, before it gets too bad". So I stopped altogether. I realised I can't do that—it's 80 bucks for a point of shard and that's nothing—it doesn't last. Now I pay 10 bucks for a gram of choof and that lasts heaps longer.

This kind of decision-making process is typical of young drug users. Young people using drugs are generally forced to be opportunistic in what they are using. Limited access to money, as well as dealers less inclined to sell to unreliable teenagers, leaves little room for preferences. Jahl was one of only five young people in the study who cited a stimulant as a primary drug of concern. Most of these young people may have had a predilection for depressants, but what these depressants were tended to depend on availability. These young people were making situated choices in their drug use, and which drug they used was subject to change. However, the choice was about which drug was most affordable or had the least ill-effects. There was less "choice" in drug use itself.

While participants were making decisions about their drug use—whether it be to use clean needles, use a drug which was less expensive, to not smoke cannabis if one had psychosis—the more problematic drug use became, the less individuals practised any legitimate decision-making. Jazmine showed insight into how this situated choice was practised as well as the meaning of making the "choice" to be reckless:

I don't have a lot of friends who do drugs, but my friends who do do drugs, they are pretty responsible about it. They will test pills and stuff like that. But I got to a point where I could just not give a shit. I would take ecstasy, snort a line of speed, do a bunch of alcohol, and I did not care at all. And that is self-harm in itself, obviously.

The point at which Jazmine's regard for her own well-being deteriorated so markedly was also the point at which her depression had flourished. There was a strong relationship between substance abuse and mental health issues, which is detailed in Chap. 4.

Discussions about drug use being a choice need to be anchored in the reality that for some of the young people in this study, drug use was not a legitimate "choice" and it was often a way to "stop thinking" about traumatic experiences in their lives over which they had had no control. Ebony started using drugs when she was 13, the same age she began living on the street:

> *Mum knew and didn't do anything. She always called me a bad kid but she doesn't [get it]. I tried to tell her why I've done what I've done is because of, you know, that man [stepdad]. Everything I have done is because of that man ... my first heavy drug—I'm talking about heroin and stuff like that—was when I was homeless. One of the girls shot it up my arm for me because I was too scared to do it myself. [I was] 13 and she did it, and I just thought, "This is so good". [It makes you] just forget everything. Shortly after I ended up having an $800 a day habit.*

Ebony's expensive "habit" soon led to street-based sex work—a means of raising funds that she felt was the most morally viable of her options (each of which was illegal). Her explanation that she was not particularly unsafe did not seem convincing as this explanation was followed with a story about a girl she was friends with who was stabbed multiple times and left for dead.

Another example where the young person had no "real" choice in their drug-use initiation was Stacey. Stacey's mother had introduced her to cannabis early in her adolescence. It was a normal and accepted practice in their daily lives. Stacey did not question it—drug use was the normal way of coping with emotions. This lesson was one she took with her for her future difficulties:

> *The pot was because of my mum, but the heroin was, um, when I started to get older and I realised that what happened when I was really young [sexual abuse from school priest] was really wrong, I didn't know how to cope with it, and I just wanted something stronger than pot to block it out ... I really liked it. I didn't have to feel or put up with any of that emotional shit.*

Few young people would presume a stronger illicit substance was required to cope with recovery from rape, but for Stacey, it was the logical pathway. The dilemma with using drugs as a way of coping with psychological distress was expressed by Roxanne: "You forget about your problems, until you become addicted to drugs, and that's a bigger problem in itself."

Conclusion

This chapter has established that these young people were in pain and the drugs were providing relief from that pain. It has focused on how young people described their lives prior to entering AOD treatment services. First, it drew attention to dramatic events and extreme risk-taking that characterised these young people's lives. Second, the chapter pointed that these adolescents were active agents in their drug choices, albeit making "situated choices" that were often constrained by factors over which they had little control. These drug choices often put them in grave danger and a number had nearly died. Most could explain why they liked drugs in a single sentence: drugs enabled them to "stop thinking about things". They were "dancing with death" to anaesthetise emotional pain.

References

Australian Institute of Health and Welfare (AIHW). (2013). *Alcohol and other drug treatment services in Australia 2011–12.* Drug treatment series 21. Cat. No. HSE139. Canberra: AIHW.

Daley, K., & Kutin, J. (2013). *Young women in youth alcohol and other drug services.* Melbourne, Australia: Youth Support + Advocacy Service.

Dwyer, J. (2013). *Drug overdose deaths in Inner North West Melbourne: YDHF & INWMML forum on pharmaceutical misuse.* Coroners Prevention Unit, Coroners Court of Victoria: Victoria. Retrieved May 18, 2014, from http://www.coronerscourt.vic.gov.au/resources/acef310e-1044-4b57-b394-94371328e3bd/cpu+-+ydhf+presentation+-+24+sep+13+-+pp97+-+final.pdf

Kutin, J., Bruun, A., Mitchell, P., Daley, K., & Best, D. (2014). *Statewide youth needs census 2013 technical report: Young people in AOD services in Victoria, Victoria-wide results.* Melbourne, Australia: Youth Support + Advocacy Service.

Newman, J. (2005). Protection though participation: Young people affected by forced migration and political crisis, *RSC Working Paper No. 20.* Refugee Studies Centre Working Paper Series: University of Oxford.

Shiner, M., & Newburn, T. (1997). Definitely, maybe not: The normalisation of recreational drug use amongst young people. *Sociology, 31*(3), 511–529.

3

The Early Years

I met the participants when they were accessing services for problematic substance use. Upon meeting them, it was not long before I could think of explanations for their substance abuse: sex work, homelessness and involvement in peer groups where drug use was common were all possible reasons. Nonetheless, I wondered if there was more to it than that—a deeper layer of explanation. I wanted to know why these young people had moved on to problematic drug use, when others who had faced similar life adversities had not. I wondered if the concept of resilience was relevant—were those who had "recovered" from their adverse experiences more resilient than those who had not?

There are many cases of young people demonstrating remarkable resilience in the face of extreme adversity. Newman (2005) studied young people living in war, which showed that even when placed in circumstances for which one cannot prepare, young people demonstrated an undeniable resilience. Psychologist Michael Ungar (2011) has undertaken considerable work on children's resiliency and argues that children can cope with immense stress, provided that their broader "social ecology" has sufficient protective factors. This is because resiliency is not an innate quality.

© The Author(s) 2016
K. Daley, *Youth and Substance Abuse*,
DOI 10.1007/978-3-319-33675-6_3

Resilience is a widely used term that has a somewhat rubbery defini-tion. Olsson et al. (2003) found that the many different definitions made the study of resilience difficult. Undertaking an analysis of literature on resilience that was relevant to youth and mental health, they found many definitions used. Ultimately, they proposed their own:

> *Resilience can be defined as a dynamic process of adaptation to a risk setting that involves interaction between a range of risk and protective factors from the individual to the social.* (p. 2)

These authors posit that rather than a fixed concept, resiliency is fluid and multifactorial. They highlight that increased protective factors can do much to ameliorate the effects of risk factors and that these factors are an interplay of individual and environmental influences. This is similar to Rutter (2012), who describes resilience as an "inter-active concept" where the presence of resilience can be witnessed by a positive outcome despite adverse circumstance. It is generally accepted that resilience is acquired through experiencing adversity (Hunter 2012). It is also accepted that resilience is not a static trait—it can both develop and dissipate in the life course (Luthar 2006; Hunter 2012).

Resilience is a trait which is shaped by both risk and protective factors in an individual's life, and it is thought that these factors are environ-mentally based. Ungar (2011) theorises resilience within a framework of "social ecology". A social ecological model looks at the connections between the social, environmental and economic aspects of an indi-vidual's life to understand them. Ungar contends that the difficulty in operationalising resiliency stems from the inability to understand how resilience can occur in situations where there are seemingly innumerable risk factors present. To redress this, he proposes that more significance be given to the influence of the social ecologies a young person is in—both social and physical—in order to understand the factors that shape resilience.

Olsson et al. (2003) suggest that rather than any adverse event itself being a single causal factor to negative outcomes, it is more instructive to look at the preceding contexts and social ecological factors in a young person's life. The nature of family relations prior to adversity is significant in predicting resilience. Olsson et al. state:

> The importance of positive parent-child attachment is a common theme in the literature. Likewise, parental warmth, encouragement and assistance, cohesion and care within the family, or a close relationship with a caring adult are commonly associated with resilient young people. (2003, p. 7)

The authors explain that family factors appear to be the strongest indicator of resilience, but other factors are also influential. Irrespective of one's academic achievement at school, school experiences with positive friendships, strong relationships with teachers and opportunities for encouragement and success all foster resilience. In a sample of 205 elementary school students, Masten et al. (1999) also found that those with more resilience had healthier peer networks and more resources than those who had "maladaptive" responses to stress and adversity.

Although there are complexities in defining a measurement of resilience, there is a consensus that both risk and protective factors influence a young person's capacity for resilience. Further, the strongest protective factor—which has the capacity to counter the most extreme life adversity—is positive relationships with family. Following this, a strong connection with peers and broader social environments such as school can buffer the likelihood of poor outcomes following traumatic life experiences. Significantly, the social environment an individual is in both prior to and following an adverse life event appears to be more influential in the development of resilience than the specific event itself (Olsson et al. 2003). This understanding of resilience is useful as we begin to unpack the early-childhood experiences of the young people in this study.

In this chapter I demonstrate that these young people's early childhoods were often filled with risk factors and relatively few protective factors. The chapter tracks participants through primary school and is narrated around their experiences of home, describing and explaining their childhoods.

Early Years

"So, tell me about your experiences of Primary School" was the first question I asked participants in the study. Purposefully broad, and reasonably impersonal, this question was left open for participants to share as much or as little as they felt comfortable. As such, it is not surprising that their responses to this question varied considerably. For some young people, primary school was wonderful and for some it was awful. Jahl's response was typical of many: "Primary school was terrible. That is a good place for you to start. Everything started there." There were some exceptions. Jess, for instance, explained that she "really excelled" in primary school, winning championships for athletics and cross-country running. Similarly, Amy "loved" her early years of school. "I never had any troubles ... I had grouse teachers and I had heaps of friends."

Having friends explained why several people liked school. As Roxanne explained, "If there's at least one person who's nice to you and is your friend, it's a lot easier to wake up in the morning and go to school." For many, an absence of friends made school an awful experience. Experiences of being bullied were common, and the effects of this permeated many aspects of participants' lives for many years. Sam was bullied through both primary and secondary school. This was often to do with his intellectual disability:

> I started getting bullied and they just made me feel really frustrated and angry and I wouldn't tell anyone ... people with a different intellectual level made me feel worse than I was ... they were a lot smarter than I was, and they could use things against me and that's when I became really depressed and upset. I'd sort of like, keep it inside ... I ended up feeling like I wanted to suicide.

In Year 7 when it became too much, Sam spoke to teachers and they, along with other workers in his life, helped him to work through this. Despite both the bullying and his intellectual disability, Sam completed school. Completing secondary education was very unusual. A more typical case is James, who was also bullied because of dyslexia but there was no intervention. Doubly disadvantaged because of dyslexia and socioeconomic disadvantage, James found the "wrong crowd" and left school by Year 10.

Eight of the young men and six of the young women had experiences of being bullied as central to their narration of school. More commonly, the absence of friends was explained by frequently moving schools. The majority of the young people in this study went to multiple schools and the main reason for shifting schools was poverty—the young person's family had to move suburbs because of financial constraints.

Poverty

By the time I met them, most participants were living well below the poverty line, and many had started life this way. Some had been middle-class with university-educated parents, but most were from working-class families who struggled financially. A significant minority of participants were raised in abject poverty, although the difficulty in measuring this categorisation makes quantifying just how many participants fell into these class categories unknown.

Some parents were able to get the bills paid each week, but this came at the cost of time with their children. Damian's father ensured the rent was always paid, but there was no money left over and his low hourly rate of pay meant that he spent very long hours at work, leaving Damian alone for long periods of time.

As well as an absence of time with a parent, poverty also meant that some young people did not have their most basic physical needs met. Ashly, who had oscillated between the care of her mother and father in Gippsland and Melbourne, described some of the daily experiences of waking up poor. When asked to discuss primary school, she recalled, "Going to school with no food. We never had food." This extreme poverty led Ashly, along with her dad and other siblings, to live on the streets. Ashly's case was unusual because she and her siblings were in the care of the father, which excluded them from women's refuges because he was male. They were also excluded from men's refuges, because children were not allowed.

Housing was a major issue for many and a significant factor in these young people's transience in schools. Maddison's family lived well below the poverty line. They were evicted from house after house, which meant that Maddison changed schools regularly. Her mother sought to make the best out of their situation—negotiating with the school principal to waive the school fees to get her children into private schools, as well as always seeking to live in "good" areas, even if it meant that the house itself was falling down. Unfortunately, Maddison felt like an outsider: "a poor kid in a rich school". Not having a blazer and holed shoes marked her as "different"' and left her on the outside of peer networks. Maddison left school at Year 10.

Ebony's family were also unable to make ends meet, and evictions were followed by Ebony switching schools. Most students did not enjoy changing schools. As Josh noted:

> *I would have preferred to stay at one primary school, because I had to make friends every time I moved to a different area and I would have to go to a new school and make new friends and it just made it a bit harder to have long-term friends.*

Having to make new friends is difficult yet integral to feeling a sense of belonging in a new school. Jessica struggled with this and found making new friends anxiety-provoking. The effects of all of this instability were unsurprising: poorer literacy, fewer friends and a permanent feeling of instability. However, it was also the smaller nuances that they spoke of which highlighted the broader effects of moving around. Despite Ashly's love of sport, she could never be involved because the constant moving around made joining a sports team unfeasible. The issue of never being engaged in a long-term school curriculum also took its toll. The inconsistent standard and curriculum across schools in separate states meant that these young people were being shifted not only between schools but also between grades. Ashly found herself in Grade Two at one school, and then Grade One at another. None of the young people had positive recollections of moving around.

Some young people who did have positive memories of primary school were those who described school as an "escape" from home. For these young people, primary school was a salvation from volatile home environments. When I asked Jai to tell me about primary school, his reply was clear: "It was an escape from home life." It did not follow that the young people who found this respite thrived at school; generally the opposite was true. Andy described primary school as "nice and fun for me", because he escaped being the victim of violence at home and, instead, became the perpetrator of it at school. Andy was expelled from several primary schools because he was a bully.

"Bad Kids"

Andy's description of himself as a "troubled child" was a sentiment shared by many others. Explaining that school was problematic was usually couched in a narrative that named the young person as the problem. For instance, Mick also had an ingrained acceptance that he was bad. "The teachers just knew that I was one of those kids that wasn't going to be the easiest ... I got expelled in primary school; that's just how school was for me."

The notion of the "kid" being "bad" was common, but as an outsider, it appeared that their "bad" behaviour always had a logical explanation. For example, Jahl's strong attachment to his mother came about after his stepfather, with whom he was very close, moved out of the family home. Jahl explained that losing his stepfather gave him a fear that he may also lose his mother and his explanation of being a "bad kid" actually just showed how this fear influenced his behaviour:

> I was just a bad kid in primary school. I wasn't so much a bad kid, I just always wanted to spend time with my mum, every recess or lunch time I would just walk home. Every time I got to school I was like, "I don't want to leave my mum" ... then every primary school I went to, I did not want to do anything. I was destructive, I would leave school—the teacher would try and stop me, and I would just push them out of the way.

In retrospect, Jahl's attachment issues seem obvious, yet at the time, the schools—of which there were several—were focused on his behaviour which was unacceptable, and Jahl was expelled more than once. As an outsider, this seems to represent a failure in how the school addressed the situation, but for Jahl, it simply reinforced his belief that he was disobedient and difficult.

A phenomenon that dominated the "bad kid" explanations was the common prevalence of a learning disability or other developmental disorder. Jahl's case above was one of many where the student's behaviour was treated as delinquency, when there was actually an underlying issue. Frequently, this was a learning difficulty. Lisa struggled with school:

> *It was harder to teach me what to do and stuff, 'cause I didn't really understand it all and then the teachers would go with the other kids who don't have difficulty learning because they find it easier to teach them, I guess … I felt like I got left out a bit in trying to learn certain things.*

Doubtless, meeting the needs of students with learning difficulties is hard in a classroom of 30 students; it is therefore not surprising that leaving these students without attention created later issues. Lizzie, for instance, was placed in a "special reading class" but despised it. Most of the children were older than Lizzie, but she still felt more advanced than them, yet behind the "mainstream" students. Lizzie explained that being bored in this class led to her acting up, which in turn further inhibited her educational development.

Alex had dyslexia but she reported her early school experiences positively, explaining that she had an integration aide which helped her enormously. This support stopped at the end of primary school, after which she "started running amok and getting into the wrong crowd".

These young people were able to identify issues which affected their education such as an absence of peers, bullying, housing instability, and abuse and neglect. Nonetheless, phrases such as "bad kid" or "not the academic type" littered their descriptions of themselves. They believed that their actions were controlled by themselves, implying that they had the potential for a brighter future should they *choose* to pursue it. It can be unwise to overemphasise to young people that their disadvantages are due to structural factors beyond their control, because it can be disempowering and dissuade them from using their agency to work towards a brighter future. Nonetheless, conceptualising a brighter future was difficult for some of these teenagers, as we shall see in the next section.

Risk Factors

It is acknowledged that the incidence of parental substance abuse is over-represented among young people who experience problematic substance use (Loxley et al. 2004). There are some explanations from a biological-determinist view which suggest a genetic disposition (Bevilacqua and Goldman 2009; Kreek et al. 2005); however, there is competing literature which argues that it is nurture, not nature, which explains the correlation. Similarly, having been raised in a home with family violence has also been identified as a risk factor for later problematic substance use (Kilpatrick et al. 2000), but the reason for this is less established. When we seek to understand why there are links between these factors we reduce the hallmarks of youth substance abuse to factors associated with individuals. While it is important to understand what specific factors individuals face, we need to be mindful that they are all symptoms of a larger affliction: poverty. Acknowledging this, we then need to consider the interplay of these factors.

Very few of the participants were raised in families with two biological parents. A few were in the primary care of their fathers, but most were with their mothers. Some had step-parents that were stable figures, but more commonly, their mothers had a "boyfriend" who rotated in identity. Marital breakdown was common, and its high prevalence among the participants in this study is, at first glance, not especially noteworthy. Many of the young people had a parent with either a severe mental health disorder or a drug issue, and violence was common in some families.

Parental Mental Illness

Thirty-five of the 61 young people spoke of a parent having a mental illness, and this was more common in women (66 per cent) than in men (48 per cent). Often young people felt responsible for their parents and did not attend school so that they could look after them, particularly when they were concerned a parent might commit suicide.

Jakey's mum had bipolar disorder, as did his auntie who had attempted suicide on several occasions. Jakey explained that he had gotten used to his mother's extreme mood swings but that it was hard to cope with and not something his friends could ever understand. His mother's mental health issues affected his own mental health in a number of ways, contributing significantly to Jakey's own battle with depression. Added to this were daily restrictions—not wanting to bring friends over, not being able to go to friends' homes because he felt a need to care for her—as well as the emotional impact of being the carer rather than the cared-for.

Similarly, Damian's mother also had bipolar disorder and was at times suicidal. When Damian was living with her, he often missed school because he feared she might kill herself. Damian was unsure of what to do. "They don't teach you this stuff at school," he lamented. This casual reflection emphasised just how deep the crevasse must have been between Damian's home life and his experiences of school.

Because of their mothers' mental health issues, neither Crystal nor Sam was ever in their primary care. Both began to have relationships with their mothers later in adolescence and almost immediately were burdened with the responsibility of protecting their mothers. Both had romanticised ideals of reuniting with their lost parent, but both just were confronted by a reality that was starkly different from their "ideal", discovering how unwell their mothers were.

Parental Substance Abuse

Parental substance use is often used as an indicator of "risk". McGlade et al. (2009) have identified mother's substance abuse as a common feature of youth in poorer outcomes for children in state care. However, it is difficult to know whether the substance use is the risk or other factors that the child experienced. The relationship is clearly more complex, but nonetheless, parental substance abuse was also a feature of many of the young people's developmental years.

Parental substance use was present for 31 participants (51 per cent), and this affected participants in different ways. Jakey, for instance, did not know that his father had a significant cannabis habit until he was 19, when he found a bag of marijuana and a stack of pornographic magazines on the inside cabin of a canoe. Jakey's father's drug use was always kept out of the house and away from the children; it was only later that his father admitted that it was a daily habit.

More typical were the cases where substance use was visible, even when this was not intended. Sometimes, substance abuse had negative impacts on people's parenting skills. Jai's mum was often out at night, leaving her children by themselves. Jai explained that his mother would come home early in the mornings "drugged up and binging on alcohol". He said that going to school "guarded" his younger siblings from the worst effects of his mother's alcohol abuse.

Attempts to hide drug use from children seemed futile. Jessica explained that her parents' separation was because her mother wanted to get the children away from their father's drug use, but not only was Jessica aware that her father's drug use was heavy, she also moved in with him in her early teen years after her mother had re-partnered with someone who was violent. Jessica still lives with her father, and while she is physically safe, his drug use makes it difficult for her to sustain a drug-free life.

Many young people were in homes of very heavy drug use. Shawn was also aware of his mother's drug use but was not encouraged to participate in this behaviour. He explained:

My mum always kept me away from her drug use—she always did everything she could [to hide it]. One time, I actually caught her with the needle in her arm and she lied to me and said that she had diabetes.

As Shawn got older, this story's improbability became clear. But his mother did not encourage or provide him with drugs. However, her inability to parent effectively because of her heavy drug use led to Shawn, and his five siblings, being placed in and out of the care of the state. Ashly, who had slept rough with her father and siblings, had earlier been removed from her mother's care for similar reasons:

We were just waking up to our mother drunk and going to sleep to her drunk. That's when my sister had to step in and take us on … She's still got my baby sister in her care. … She's only 24. She's been doing this since she was 13.

For Ashly and others, the heavy use of drugs within the family created an environment where drug use was an accepted and expected family practice. These young people were often using drugs for lengthy periods before they realised that their drug use might be an issue. For many of them, drug use was not a choice or a leisure activity; it was a part of everyday life.

Physical Violence

As well as substance use and mental health issues, family violence dominated the biographies of participants' early years. For Anthony, alcohol and other drug use inflamed his stepfather's violence. Often the house was smashed up entirely. Brandon was the youngest child of three brothers and they were raised watching their father beat their mother:

> *Dad just used to come home and flip out. Mum's had broken bones and everything. She's gone through hell ... I used to run into my room and sit on my door and push it back and just hide because Dad used to beat her hard. But one of my brothers used to stand around and make sure that he didn't do anything too serious. But they were only 17 when it was happening so they were getting a flogging too.*

Shawn's mother had many boyfriends, all of whom were violent. Shifting from one violent relationship to the next, there were many periods when the family would have to flee without notice, which meant that Shawn's school attendance was infrequent and interspersed with long periods of absence:

> *I'd go one day, and then I couldn't go for a month because my stepdad belted my mum and we'd be staying in a domestic violence place, or we'd have to move house, or some other reason ... my stepdad was very violent ... he was actually charged with the attempted murder of me and my mum.*

Young people spoke about their experiences of violence matter-of-factly. Shawn's casual follow-up that his stepfather tried to murder him was treated as an almost unremarkable part of his story. This attitude was typical, especially so among the young men. Andy explained some of the daily grind of his experience:

There was a lot of family violence when I was younger. A lot of family issues, break-ups, house moving ... you go to school, but then you don't want to come home because you know you are going to get belted when you come home.

Andy described how after being slapped on bare skin by his stepfather, his skin was bruised for a week—he was told to not show anyone at school.

The normalisation of violence in the home was common. For instance, when I asked Cameron how primary school was, he reported that it was good and that he had a stable home and family around him. Then he said, "I suppose there was some bad things." This was soon followed by a dispassionate explanation that his dad used to abuse him and "shit like that". Cameron recalled the violence as "normal".

For Alex, violence was also part of "normal" family life. Her stepfather's violence was discussed as something trivial:

I remember my stepdad picking me up and chucking me against the wall. Just little things like that. Nothing like full physical.

Adult men role-modelling violence was not unique. As well as her stepdad, Alex's biological father was also violent. He beat his pregnant partner so severely that she was hospitalised. Alex described the assault as inconsequential: "a few bruises". The tendency to diminish the severity of violence did not differ across genders. Gerald described his childhood as having both physical and emotional abuses but qualified this by saying that he had "heard worse" stories than his. It was as though Gerald felt guilty for mentioning such an inane point.

Experiences of extreme physical violence were common. Many of the young men carried with them permanent injuries from childhood abuse. The extent of head trauma Anthony suffered has resulted in the permanent loss of his olfactory senses. Gerald was unable to straighten his legs properly because the physical assaults in the home so early on in his life had damaged his skeletal development. Yet despite the extremity of the violence they experienced, it was perceived as a routine part of growing up by the participants themselves: they had never experienced a world free from violence.

The normalisation of violence in the home led to a normalisation of violence more generally. Andy explained the details of his stepfather's physical assaults and then concluded that:

> *I knew I was getting bashed because I needed it. If I didn't cop it, I would have been ten times worse than I already am and I know that for a fact because I have matured and stuff.*

We see that Andy's understanding of the abuse was not that he was a victim of it but that he deserved it and became better for it. Such an understanding of family violence likely serves two purposes: (1) it enables Andy to be an autonomous agent, in that if he chose to behave differently, he would not receive the abuse. Therefore, violence was a consequence of his actions rather than his stepfather's. The follow-on from this is that it empowers the individual to believe that they are able to end the violence should they begin to behave differently; (2) it helps Andy to reconcile that tension between having received abuse from a person tasked with his protection. While these may be hypotheses, we can see clearly that Andy accepted violence as a necessary part of life.

Sexual Violence

Many participants were also victims of sexual violence. This was much more prevalent among the young women, but also to be expected is the under-reporting of sexual abuse among the young men. Jessica was raised in a home where abuse of all forms were inescapable. Her mother's dependence on her abusive stepfather added more emotional pain to Jessica's daily experience of violence and rape. After they finally fled the violence and received housing from a women's service, Jessica's mother resumed contact with him. She explained to Jessica it was for the sake of her younger half-sister; nonetheless, things downward-spiralled rapidly:

> *Then he started giving Mum drugs and money and shouting at her all the time. She started bringing him to the house, and he wasn't allowed at the house. She only had that house because she was getting away from him and she promised*

she wouldn't bring him to the house. Then she starting having sex with him and she was like, "Oh, we're just having a bit of fun" … she kicked me out and told me that us kids stole the best years of her life and she wishes she never had us.

When Lisa spoke about her physically abusive stepfather, she recalled when it first began: "He grabbed me a bit one day and my mum just stood there and watched it and didn't try to stop it." In cases where the mother knew of the abuse, her failure to act was deeply troubling for the young people.

Amber was sexually abused by her father, as too were her brothers. She was the youngest, and only later did her older brothers confide in her that their father also used to have "friends" come over and sexually abuse them when the mother was out drinking. Amber felt a deep injustice that her father had not been punished for what he had done:

I wish my father was six-foot under the ground. Heaps of people know about my life and they wish that too. Fuck it. But my brother, apparently he went psychotic and he went into the cop station and told them everything about my father, and he still hasn't been locked away for it—he should be in jail for what he has done to me and my brothers. I just reckon it's so unfair.

Amber recalled that when she was about five, upon hearing that her father had had a heart attack, she replied to her mother, "I hope he dies." Even Amber acknowledged that this was a very extreme thing for a small child to say. She explained that it was an instinctive reaction to all of the abuse. "I'd just been belted up that much and touched and that."

Young people were traumatised by their experiences of abuse and neglect, but also by the absence of protection. The inaction of their non-abusive parent scarred them deeply. Lucinda was sexually abused by her brother, which was something that her mother refused to accept:

My mum told me it was a dream. When I was five I brought it up with her and she was like, "Oh, it was just a dream".

Lucinda was eventually placed into the care of the state, but there were also cases where abuse was hidden from the authorities.

Ebony was sexually abused by her stepfather, while her brother suffered extreme psychological abuse from both his mother and stepfather. They would serve his dinner in a dog bowl on the driveway and make him eat and sleep outside. Bearing witness to this had effects on Ebony:

> *[It was] really hard, extremely hard. It was just hard because I was younger, I didn't know a lot of the services. I didn't know what I could do, and they are people who, when you put people in front of the household, they'd look like perfect parents. But behind, they were evil. I've had DoCS [Department of Community Services] over once, and they just acted like the perfect parents so they left and didn't do anything.*

State Care

> *I felt very lost. Very, very lost. I needed rules. I needed a mum, I needed a dad. I needed stability and someone to help me.—Jess*

Interventions from the state were a vexed issue. There were 32 (53 per cent) young people who had been in state care, but there were many others where one wonders why the state had not been involved. Young people who had been in care, and those who had not, expressed concerns about the child protection system; however, all agreed that there is a need for child protective services. Nonetheless, being removed from the family and placed into the care of "The State" came with many issues.

Similar to other Australian states and territories, in Victoria, in order for the child protection services to become involved in a family, there needs to be "notifications" made to them. The number of notifications required to warrant a home visit depends on the nature of the notification as well as the age of the child. Once at the home, the social worker makes an assessment as to whether or not the notifications are substantiated. In Ebony's case, there were several reports to the Department of Community Services (DoCS) for them to send a social worker out to her home, but given that there were no infants in the home whose lives were at imminent risk this rarely amounted to anything. Despite Ebony's desperation to be rescued, this led to no further contact and she continued to live in an abusive household. Ebony reflected on what could have been an alternate outcome the day the worker came to her home:

> Just believe us—what's the use of us lying? They should have put us in a refuge overnight and just went from there. You know, at least got some counselling that the family had to abide by. For the whole family—relationship counselling. I wish they had of put something in place rather than just walk away.

Ebony's suggestion that family counselling and monitoring would have assisted highlights just how reluctant children are to be removed from their families. She was the victim of multiple forms of abuse at home and eventually ran away. During her time on the streets, Ebony came to the attention of an outreach service attached to state care. She was placed in residential care, which she often absconded from. At 16 Ebony was exited from care back to her mother's, where her stepfather again sexually assaulted her. Soon after, she was back sleeping on the streets. Nonetheless, even years later and now separated from her family entirely, she still suggests that working on remedying the issues within the family, rather than simply removing her from them, would have been the ideal course of action.

There were many pathways into the care of the state, but the defining feature was that the transition was rarely linear. For example, Luke first went into foster care after his mother placed an intervention order against him. His father had refused to accommodate him, but after only one night in care, his father changed his mind. However, after two months with his dad things broke down and Luke was again placed in care before he began couch-surfing.

There are three key types of care in Victoria. *Foster care* is where a young person is placed in the home of a registered foster parent and their family. The younger the child, the more likely they are to be placed in foster care. However, there is a significant undersupply of foster-carers. Where there are no available carers, or the young person has needs that are too great for a foster care placement, they are placed in *residential care*. This is where a child lives in a staffed residence with approximately three or four other children. The staff change regularly and there is typically no "parent" figure. Children here have freedoms such as being able to come and go as they please; however, these freedoms come with costs, such as not having a regular face to come home to for a hug. It is somewhat paradoxical that children with greater needs are placed into group homes, as it would seem probable that they are most in need of intensive one-on-one support. Finally, there is *secure welfare*, where young people are mandated to be placed in when it has been established that they pose too high a risk to themselves or others. As the name suggests, it is a secured residence where young people are detained.

For some, the circumstances surrounding the removal from the family were so traumatic that it seems improbable for state care to have any prospect of being positive. Ashly, for instance, was removed from her mother's care on many occasions and recalls these uncomfortably:

> *It was scary. 'Cause my mum's always going off her head, Dad was never there. It was always after a big night of drinking or something. Every time my mum got drunk, she's got a big mouth, so she always got bashed and we'd be getting dragged into the car by DHS and police and mum's going off her head, pissin' out blood.*

These care placements were always temporary, which exacerbated the feeling of volatility and instability in her life:

> *They used to come and grab us ... most of the times they used to take us together, but sometimes they'd separate us ... but we were only there for two or three weeks at the most, then mum would go fix herself up and be straight in court and then she'd get us back straight away.*

When Ashly was in her first year of high school, she was removed from her mother's care permanently and placed in the care of her older sister. We see later that this did not mean Ashly was consistently housed: at many times over the years she and her siblings slept rough.

For other young people, well-intended efforts to avoid removal failed, and during the period of trying to find a sustainable outcome, the young person's well-being deteriorated. Jess was one such case. After eventually being removed from her mother's care, she spent two years in different residential units before being placed into kinship care with her grand-parents. By this point, Jess had many emotional and behavioural issues:

> *[By] the time they got me, I was haywire. My heart and head were doing two different things. My head was like, "I will do whatever the fuck I want", because I had been in resi-units for two years; and my heart was telling me that I was still their little princess and that I should be doing housework and helping my grandparents … we fought.*

Jess was then placed into foster care with a woman whom she became quite close with. However, Jess's biological mother was still her legal guardian and she vetoed this arrangement. Jess's mother was enraged that Jess appeared to be thriving under the maternal instincts of another. She told Jess that if she was not going to be a "good girl" for her at home—where a "good girl" required submitting to the sexual desires of her step-father—then no one else could have her. Jess was subsequently placed back into residential units. Jess still has the "family photo" with her foster family.

These convoluted pathways through care emphasised the already marked absence of stability of structure in these young people's lives. There is a distinct tension between removing children from abuse, but at the same time inflicting so many traumas in the experience of removal that children are irreparably damaged.

Experiences in State Care

As discussed, 32 of the young people had been in the care and protection system. This was much more prevalent among females, with 69 per cent having contact with child protection services compared with 40 per cent of males. Some children were on supervision orders but remained in the monitored care of their family; others were placed into alternate care arrangements, typically residential units with other young people, often after multiple foster placements. This is not typical of young people in the care of the state. Only a small percentage of children in care are in residential care; most are placed in foster families.

The Australian Institute of Health and Welfare (AIHW) provides an annual report on child protection figures in Australia, with information collated from each of the states and territories. The 2013–14 report indicates that at 6.0 per 1000 children, Victoria has the lowest rate of children in care, with the national rate being 8.1 per 1000. Only 6 per cent of children in care in Victoria reside in residential care, with 79 per cent living in either foster care or kinship care and 15 per cent in "other/unknown" accommodation (AIHW 2015). While most young people in care reside with foster families, we have seen that young people in this study who had been in state care had all been in residential units. Some of them had been in foster care first. While state-care involvement was a factor which was vastly over-represented in this sample, it is also true that this over-representation was from a small minority within the care system.

The common perception of child protection systems is that they are inadequate and often cause more harm than that which they seek to prevent, often because of a lack of good policy and process (Cook 2014; Hall 2015; McDonald 2015; Scarr 2015). Child protection services are typically perceived as failing to care for those whose protection they are tasked with: seeing children's well-being deteriorate rather than improve, and much literature has found very poor outcomes for young care leavers in the domains of mental health (Percora et al. 2009), involvement with the justice system (Mendes et al. 2014) and substance use (Baidawi and Mendes 2010; Daley and Chamberlain 2009).

For some participants, this was the case—especially those who were placed into residential care, which was almost universally described as a breeding ground for drug use and crime. However, there is a concurrent narrative to this negative construction. Some of the young people who had been in the care of the state provided a description of what it was like. On one hand, they were able to identify problems and shortcomings but, on the other, were equally able to identify the positive aspects.

Habib entered the care system when he was 16 and placed into foster care. He enjoyed this but repeatedly ran away from his placement. He was then placed into secure welfare, where young people are detained involuntarily after being assessed as too high a risk to self or others. Habib also liked this. The experience of enjoying state care was an unexpected narrative. I enquired what he liked about it:

> *Everything. You can eat whatever you want; you can go out; you get seven smokes a day—they look after your smokes; you get your own shower; you get your own bed. You can do whatever! You've got the gym, you've got computers, you've got a basketball court—you've got everything.*

This quote tells much more than what Habib liked about state care: it also illuminates what he did not have at home. Few young people are likely to list having their own bed as a reason to appreciate accommodation that involuntarily detains them and significantly restricts freedoms. Things like food and a bed are (rightly) taken-for-granted aspects of home life for young people, but a typical home life was absent in these young people's lives.

The appeal of state care as a "home" was also echoed by Lisa:

> *I kind of liked the resi-unit—there was heaps of food … I kind of liked it in there because it felt a bit stable. I felt safe in a stable place, a little bit.*

Lisa and her best friend had come into contact with Streetworks—the child protection street outreach team—when they were 14 and sleeping rough:

> *They saw us hanging around people … seeing these two girls always hanging around older people. I don't know, they think you're at risk. And they're probably right … I didn't feel at risk at the time; I just thought it was fun.*

Jahl also came into contact with child protection during his time on the streets. The police would pick him up on the streets and, upon discovering that he was homeless, arrange for DHS to place him into residential care. Jahl was happy to have somewhere to stay and recollected his first placement almost identically to Habib: "We could do whatever we wanted—we could eat food. We'd wake up and eat food!"

The common reason young people enjoyed care was because there was food and because they were safe. Lizzie had many negative things to say about her time in care but was adamant that the safety and stability it provided was much needed. My early surprise that participants enjoyed state care was perhaps not so much a reflection on my misunderstandings of the care system but my misunderstandings as to how dire their home lives had been.

Despite these positive experiences, not all care placements were equal. After his first experience which was positive, Jahl also encountered hostile, unsafe and uncaring placements:

> *It smelled like Juvie and I just did not like it. One of the workers caught me with choof and then hated me since then. We nearly punched on. He was like egging me on, "Fucking hit me," and I was like, "What the fuck? Are you serious?" … I made seven complaints because all of the workers turned on me and this other kid that was living there. We were shit-stirring them, but they fully turned on us. I got out of care after that—I didn't like it.*

Jahl "got out of care" by getting into homelessness.

Many young people had negative recollections of being involved in child protective services, and this was always because they did not feel cared for. Stevie loathed foster care, yet conceded that "it was still better than living with my mother". But she reported feeling like a "number being pushed around on a piece of paper … No one was listening to me; no one was helping me … I just felt like some forgotten kid". Feeling as a "kid in the system" rather than someone's child was a sentiment which resonated with many even when there were positive experiences in care. Kate felt that her being placed into care was "probably a good thing", but she also added, "I don't think that they prepare you very well for leaving care though." Poor transitions out of care have been a key theme in literature on children in care in Australia (Mendes 2009; Mendes et al. 2011). It is well established that the outcomes of young people in care are poor. Johnson et al. (2010) interviewed 77 care leavers aged 18–25. They found that only 45 per cent of care leavers had secure housing post leaving care, and substance abuse problems were also prevalent for 53 per cent of the young people in their study. Further to this, 53 per cent of the sample did not complete their senior years of secondary education. Similarly, Osborn and Bromfield (2007) reviewed eight substantive studies on outcomes of leaving care and found that care leavers were over-represented on virtually all indicators of disadvantage, including substance use, mental health issues, housing instability, poor employment outcomes and offending behaviours.

Participants' experiences and views on care and protection differed. What is noteworthy is that they were aware of the dilemmas involved in their situations and, in light of that, did not dismiss the role of child protection entirely. Some young people spoke of child protection positively, while other were contemptuous; however, all were aware that there was a need for the state to be involved in their lives. Removing children from the care of their parents—regardless of how warranted it may be—is a traumatising experience for the child and makes the relevant authorities arbiters of very precarious decisions. Balancing the tension between protecting young people, while not further traumatising them, is inherently difficult.

This section has shown that there were consistent positive responses to state care—safety, stability and food. Notwithstanding, there were also significant problems. Some of these issues could be addressed with programmatic solutions, but the deepest concern that came with being placed in care was not something service providers could escape. As the formal name, "Out of Home Care", suggests, it does not substitute a "home". Lisa captured this sentiment well:

> It's a stable place, but if you don't have the affection from a parent and everything like that, you are an outcast in the world.

Conclusion

This chapter began by pointing out that both risk and protective factors influence a young person's capacity for resilience. Further, the strongest protective factor—which has the capacity to counter the most extreme life adversity—is positive relationships with family. This chapter has tracked participants through their early childhood narrated through their experiences of home.

There were indicators in early childhood that these young people were at risk. Most grew up in homes that were without safe and secure attachments, where abuse and neglect were common. Parents failed to provide these young people with consistent affection and emotional security that encourage pro-social development and foster resiliency. Half (53 per cent) of the young people were in contact with the state care and protection system and half (47 per cent) were not, although this is not necessarily indicative of their needs. Either pathway had its own issues, with those in care feeling uncared for and those not in care often suffering in silence. The research on resiliency (see especially: Ungar 2011, 2013) helps us to understand that many young people are able to overcome extreme adversity, but they need to have at least one positive adult in their life who provides consistent support and emotional security.

The more I explored young people's early childhood, the clearer it became that for many it was not a single adversity that characterised their early lives but a barrage of adversities that they had to face without consistent love and support from parents. These young people did not have a safe home or even a safe person in their lives. There was no adult to help them develop the resiliency needed to deal with the challenges and disappointments that life throws up. In many ways, these young people had spent much of their early lives not trying to "overcome" adversity but working out how to live with it.

References

Australian Institute of Health and Welfare (AIHW). (2015). Child protection Australia: 2013–14. Child Welfare series no. 61. Cat. no. CWS 52. Canberra: AIHW.

Baidawi, S., & Mendes, P. (2010). Young people transitioning from out-of-home care and problematic substance use: The views of young people and workers in Victoria. *Children Australia, 35*(4), 23–30.

Bevilacqua, L., & Goldman, D. (2009). Genes and addictions. *Clinical Pharmacology and Therapeutics, 85*(4), 59–361.

Cook, H. (2014, March 26). System failing children in state care: Auditor-general John Doyle. *The Age.* Retrieved March 14, 2016, from http://www.theage.com.au/victoria/system-failing-children-in-state-care-auditorgeneral-john-doyle-20140326-35htf.html

Daley, K., & Chamberlain, C. (2009). Moving on: Young people and substance abuse. *Youth Studies Australia, 28*(4), 35–43.

Hall, B (2015, May 27). "Systemic deficiencies": Auditor-general slams DHHS child protection failures. *The Age.* Retrieved March 14, 2016, from http://www.theage.com.au/victoria/systemic-deficiencies-auditorgeneral-slams-dhhs-child-protection-failures-20150527-ghajzp.html

Hunter, C. (2012). *Is resilience still a useful concept when working with children and young people?* Melbourne, Australia: Australian Institute of Family Studies. Retrieved February 26, 2014, from http://www.aifs.gov.au/cfca/pubs/papers/a141718/cfca02.pdf

Johnson, G., Natalier, K., Mendes, P., Liddiard, M., Thoresen, S., Hollows, A., et al. (2010). *Pathways from out-of-home care.* AHURI Final Report; no. 147. Australian Housing and Urban Research Institute: Melbourne, Australia.

Kilpatrick, D. G., Acierno, R., Saunders, B., Resnick, H. S., Best, C. L., & Schnurr, P. P. (2000). Risk factors for adolescent substance abuse and dependence from a national sample. *Journal of Consulting and Clinical Psychology, 68*(1), 19–30.

Kreek, M. J., Nielsen, D. A., Butelman, E. R., & LaForge, K. S. (2005). Genetic influences on impulsivity, risk taking, stress responsivity and vulnerability to drug abuse and addiction. *Nature Neuroscience, 8,* 1450–1457.

Loxley, W., Toumbourou, J. W., Stockwell, T., Haines, B., Scott, K., Godfrey, C., et al. (2004). *The prevention of substance use, risk and harm in Australia: A review of the evidence.* Canberra, Australia: Australian Government Department of Health and Ageing.

Luthar, S. S. (2006). Resilience in development: A synbook of research across five decades. In D. Chiccetti & D. Cohen (Eds.), *Developmental psychopathology: Risk, disorder and adaptation* (pp. 739–795). New York: John Wiley & Sons.

Masten, A. S., Hubbard, J. J., Gest, S. D., Tellegen, A., Garmezy, N., & Ramirez, M. (1999). Competence in the context of adversity: Pathways to resilience and maladaptation from childhood to late adolescence. *Development and Psychopathology, 11,* 143–169.

McDonald, P. (2015, August 23). Out-of-home care is failing Victoria's most vulnerable children. *The Age.* Retrieved March 14, 2016, from http://www.smh.com.au/comment/outofhome-care-is-failing-victorias-most-vulnerable-children-20150820-gj3x0x.html

McGlade, A., Ware, R., & Crawford, M. (2009). Child protection outcomes for infants of substance-using mothers: A matched-cohort study. *Pediatrics, 124*(1), 285–293.

Mendes, P. (2009). Young people transitioning from state out-of-home care: Jumping hoops to access employment. *Family Matters, 83*, 32–38.

Mendes, P., Baidawi, S., & Snow, P. (2014). Young people transitioning from out-of-home care: A critical analysis of leaving care policy, legislation and housing support in the Australian state of Victoria. *Child Abuse Review, 23*(6), 402–414.

Mendes, P., Johnson, G., & Moslehuddin, B. (2011). *Young people leaving state out-of-home care: Australian policy and practice*. Melbourne, Australia: Australian Scholaraly Publishing.

Newman, J. (2005). Protection though participation: Young people affected by forced migration and political crisis, *RSC Working Paper No. 20*. Refugee Studies Centre Working Paper Series: University of Oxford.

Olsson, C. A., Bond, L., Burns, J. M., Vella-Brodrick, D. A., & Sawyer, S. M. (2003). Adolescent resilience: A concept analysis. *Journal of Adolescence, 26*, 1–11.

Osborn, A., & Bromfield, L. (2007). Young people leaving care. *National Child Protection ClearingHouse Research Brief 7*. Australian Institute of Family Studies: Melbourne, Australia.

Percora, P. J., White, C. R., Jackson, L. J., & Wiggins, T. (2009). Mental health of current and former recipients of foster care: A review of recent studies in the USA. *Child and Family Social Work, 14*(132), 146.

Rutter, M. (2012). Resilience as a dynamic concept. *Development and Psychopathology, 24*(2), 335–344.

Scarr, L. (2015, April 16). Revealed: The hell Aussie kids in out-of-home care are living in. *The Daily Telegraph*. Retrieved March 14, 2016, from http://www.dailytelegraph.com.au/news/national/revealed-the-hell-aussie-kids-in-outofhome-care-are-living-in/news-story/4f51a297e0b9b4e41ddb8daccce73d97

Ungar, M. (2011). The social ecology of resilience: Addressing contextual and cultural ambiguity of a nascent construct. *American Journal of Orthopsychiatry, 81*(1), 1–17.

Ungar, M. (2013). The impact of youth-adult relationships on resilience. *International Journal of Child, Youth and Family Studies, 3*, 328–336.

4

In the Mix: The Beginning of a Drug Problem

Many of the young men and women in this study had "troubled child-hoods", but this does not explain why they developed a substance abuse problem in their teenage years. Troubled childhoods do not necessarily *cause* substance abuse, so I wanted to investigate the pathway between early childhood disadvantage and adolescent substance abuse. The chapter focuses on how young people became disconnected from three integral structures in their lives: school, family and housing. Understanding the interconnections between these things is important in understanding how substance use becomes a problem. In their much-cited work, Elliott et al. (1989) highlighted that while individual factors of "risk" for young people (such as substance abuse, child abuse, mental health) had large bodies of literature, there was no literature examining what the relationship was between these factors—what the frequency of multiple risk factors was, what the temporal order of events was or what these factors meant for someone's development. This remains true today.

In this chapter I seek to describe how participants transitioned from substance use to substance abuse. I begin this chapter with young people's experiences of secondary education where they had their first initiation with alcohol and other drugs. From here we see how, for the vast majority

© The Author(s) 2016
K. Daley, *Youth and Substance Abuse*,
DOI 10.1007/978-3-319-33675-6_4

of the young people, leaving school and separation from family occurred at roughly the same time, leading to unemployment and homelessness. This critical juncture was a catalyst for heavy drug use and poor mental health.

There were six young people who had never been homeless, and an account on their pathway into problematic drug use is also provided at the end of the chapter. I conclude that while there was not a single specific pathway from childhood trauma to substance abuse, there were key factors—leaving school, separation from family, unemployment and homelessness—that were usually "in the mix".

High School

Fifty-six of the 61 young people began high school. The five who did not begin high school had many similarities: all were male, all had been in state care, all had a mental health issue, all had a parent with a substance abuse issue and all but one had a parent with a mental health issue. Thus, despite being legally required to be enrolled in education until they are 16, their non-attendance in secondary education was undetected. School attendance and enrolment are largely the responsibility of the parents. In these cases, the parents had little attention on and/or interest in their child's participation in education. All but one of these young men ended up involved in the criminal justice system.

Among the rest of the sample, there was uneven engagement with secondary education. Sixty-two per cent attended more than one high school and a third went to more than three high schools. The persistent shifting of schools was typically associated with the issues outlined in the previous chapter. For instance, domestic violence saw families relocate, and likewise, those placed in state care were often in temporary placement, and with each shift in care placement came a shift in schools.

In the last chapter we saw that many of the young people had learning difficulties and this issue was central to their memories of primary school. This issue resurfaced in their discussion of secondary education. James did not know he was dyslexic until he was in high school. While late, it did offer an explanation for his extreme difficulty through primary school. Insufficiently literate, he left the mainstream school he was enrolled in for a school catering for young people who had learning disabilities. James's experience of school improved considerably when he was in an environment where his needs were identified and addressed. Ally also struggled in a mainstream school and found that her emotional and social needs were better met at an alternative school; however, her academic needs were not. She found herself bored and then left school permanently.

Shifting schools was a common experience in both primary and secondary schools. Girls were more likely to have had a consistent school experience in primary school, with 50 per cent having attended just one school, whereas only 31 per cent of boys were at the same school from prep through to Year 6. In high school, this pattern was reversed, with only 31 per cent of girls remaining at the same school, compared with 43 per cent of boys. Notably, more than half of the young people had attended multiple secondary schools, with one-third of the young people having been to three or more high schools. Unstable home environments combined with the frequent displacement between schools laid a poor foundation for academic success. There is no single explanation for why those who truant and/or leave school early are more likely to have substance abuse issues. Nonetheless, there is certainly a relationship between being disconnected from school and youthful drug use. These are two issues, among others, which contribute to an overall sense of disaffection among young people (Newburn and Shiner 2005).

Jess had been sexually abused by her stepfather and this became known to the authorities. One day in Year 7, Jess arrived home from school to find the police and child protection workers at her house. Jess was removed from the care of her parents and placed into the care of the state. Child protection were unable to find a permanent placement and Jess shifted between temporary foster placements and residential units. This explained why she had attended seven secondary schools. When I asked her how she found shifting around all the time, she replied: "Well my education was fucked up—it was very holey."

Drug Use Initiation

For the majority of participants, their first experience of substance use came during secondary school. For most, initiation was with friends, but for a significant minority, drugs were first offered by a family member. For young people in the care of the state, drug use was the norm. Ebony's early drug use was reasonably typical of most:

> *I started smoking marijuana, hanging around the wrong people, peer pressure … I didn't have many friends, so I thought, "This is great having friends!"*

It was not just drug use that connected Ebony to her new friends. Among other young drug users, she found a shared understanding:

> *[It was good] having friends and people to hang out with and talk to. People who related to my family environment—[It helped] to get that off my chest.*

Ebony alludes to her inability to disclose her family background to her mainstream peers. However, she was able to disclose it to others who had similar life experiences. The benefits of having friends she could talk to, as well as taking part in shared recreational activities, was appealing, though drug use was a normative social practice of this group.

Josh was having difficulties coping with school. He was asked to leave several schools and struggled to make friends. He left the mainstream education system when he was 13 and tried an alternative school but left by Year 10. Upon leaving school, he started smoking cannabis and through this activity he started to build friendships with other young men. He explained that he would "get baked first thing in the morning and then go to town and hang out with my mates at the park smoking".

For some participants, drug use was a normal family practice and this is where first initiation took place. Jessica said:

> *My mum and stepdad always smoked bongs and that was just normal, them smoking at the kitchen table, around the house. So I grew up thinking that when I was a teenager, I would smoke bongs and cigarettes, because that's just what you did … I first started using at Dad's.*

Young people who were raised in homes where drug use was a normal family practice often followed in their parents' footsteps.

Ashly's family were heavy drug users, and while this may have normalised drug use, we can see Ashly exercising agency and making choices about which drugs she would use:

I started smoking choof when I was about 10 or 11 … I was hanging around the city and had all my mates there … I was always the straight one [not drinking alcohol] and in the end I just thought, "Fuck it! If you can't beat 'em, join 'em!" But I didn't start off on the smack straight away—I started off on speed and then moved onto heroin. But still, it's all fucked.

Growing up on the street amidst a backdrop of heavy injecting heroin use, Ashly initially rejected intravenous drug use. She had watched her father and sister use heroin, and she was determined not to make this "choice". However, she eventually adopted the drug-using practices of her peers and heroin became her primary drug of concern.

Some participants could not escape from environments where there was widespread drug use. Matt was small in stature and was resistant to trying drugs; however, at 16 he was living in a refuge and he needed allies in the all-male accommodation. He was able to make friends, but a tacit condition of entry to this group was that he participate in drug use with them. While initially reluctant to smoke marijuana, Matt soon found this an effective way to forget about the pain of his abusive childhood. When asked what he liked about drugs, Matt said, "It made me feel good … I didn't really think about stuff."

Others who had been in state care found substance use and friendship a welcoming combination. When Jess was put into residential units, "chroming" (inhaling paint) was widespread. Staff in her unit often remarked how impressive it was that Jess continued to attend school. Eventually, their expectations were fulfilled when Jess left school in Year 10 and her drug use became entrenched. State care and parental substance use were not the only entry points into drug use. Voni explained that she had a loving family and did okay at school. Voni was using heroin while she was still at school:

I would go into the cubicles and have a hit, then come back in class and go on the nod. I remember once, this specific day, I went and had a hit in the toilet and came back ... I passed her [the teacher] a piece of paper and she clearly saw my arms [with blood from a recent injection], and you know, nothing was ever done about it. That's when I first started using.

I wondered if there had been a significant event in her life that made the pain-killing properties of opiates desirable. When I asked about traumatic events in her life, she replied: "Well I started using drugs after I was sexually assaulted." Voni had been raped by someone she knew in high school. The school was unaware of this, but at least one teacher knew of her drug use. Voni received neither care nor intervention and eventually she left school completely.

School Separation

We can see that by this point young people were on the margins at school. Shifting from school to school, as well as initiation into substance use, only served to widen the gap between them and formal education. Kate was in the care of the state and went to six high schools. She was in temporary foster placements and then residential care, which led to her moving homes and schools every few months. Three years into high school (Year 9) she left school completely.

Cameron had an abusive home life. When asked what he liked about school, he said that it was an "escape" from home. However, despite school providing him with a safe haven, he was "acting-up" and was kicked out of school when he was 14. Immediately after being expelled from school, his father expelled him from home. Overnight, Cameron became homeless and was disconnected from school and his peers. Not surprisingly, this did not bode well for him. While at times there appeared to be a whole life of traumatic events that led to young people's drug use, it also appeared to happen very quickly once there was disconnection from key people or structures in their lives.

Lizzie had been bullied through primary school, which continued in high school. She was placed into state care when she was in Year 10. Just days after entering care, Lizzie, aged 15, met a man aged 40, who lived nearby. On their first "date" he injected her with heroin. Their relationship continued for many years, as did their heroin use. Lizzie soon developed a "habit" and left school in Year 11.

Michael was the sole protagonist in his narrative of school—there was no reference to his parents or other caregivers in his explanation of how he "just kinda got out of the habit" of attending. Michael thought he was solely responsible for his exit from school and made no reference to any contextual factors that influenced his decision. Once he left school, his substance use escalated dramatically:

> [I was] smoking heaps of pot ... It just took up heaps of time. The whole day would be gone and I wouldn't realise. Weeks would just go by and I wouldn't realise.

The transition from substance use to substance abuse happened swiftly once young people were disconnected from school. A surplus of time, and few positive or purposeful things to do, made drug use appealing. An environment where it was normalised made it available.

Table 4.1 shows that only 9 per cent of the young men and 15 per cent of the young women completed Year 12. The young people who completed Year 12 were atypical for a number of reasons. Jerry was a private school rebel. After being expelled from three elite private schools, he went on to thrive in a public school and did very well in his final year of education despite his drug use. However, he had a safe home and loving relationship with his parents who were financially secure.

Table 4.1 Educational outcomes by gender

Year level completed	Males %	Females %	Total %
12	9	15	12
11	6	0	3
10	20	31	25
9	26	15	21
8	17	19	18
7	9	19	13
6	14	0	8
Total	101[a]	99*	100

[a]Totals do not add up to 100 per cent because of rounding

Lucinda also completed school and was accepted to do an events management course at TAFE. Lucinda's middle-class, university-educated parents were "role models" which most participants did not have. While both Lucinda and Jerry had issues in their childhoods, they had been raised in homes where completing school was expected and there were some family supports.

These exceptions aside, early school leaving was the norm in this sample. This is despite more than 80 per cent of young people of comparable age completing secondary education (Year 12) (DEECD 2013). School is legally compulsory for everyone in Victoria until they reach 16 years of age (Year 10). However, half (53 per cent) of the girls had left school before Year 10 (Table 4.1), and another one-third (31 per cent) left at the end of Year 10 or early in Year 11.

The figures for the boys were even more dramatic: two-thirds (66 per cent) of the boys had left school before Year 10 and another one-fifth (20 per cent) left school at the end of Year 10 or early in Year 11. In fact, Table 4.1 shows that more boys left at the end of primary school (Grade 6) than completed their secondary education (14 per cent compared with 9 per cent).

As we have seen, half of the girls and two-thirds of the boys did not complete Year 10. Their pathways out of school usually had the following characteristics: they had a disrupted experience of primary school that prepared them poorly for secondary school; many of them found it difficult to "fit in" or make friends at their new school; they felt like "outsiders" because they came from families where there had been poverty, abuse, neglect and family disruption. To be an "outsider" is a considerable burden at such a young age. In search of friends, they found kindred spirits in the "wrong crowd". They began behaving badly, often failing academically. Some were expelled, others were "advised" to find a "more suitable" school and some simply "got out of the habit" of attending.

Truanting turning into complete separation from school was common. Amy had been smoking a lot of cannabis at home and stopped getting up each day to go to school. She explained her reason for leaving school in Year 11: "I was smoking and just lost my way."

Jessica was also smoking a lot of cannabis at home:

I was starting to get depression and anxiety and I didn't know, or understand, why I was feeling that way. I was arguing with Mum a lot, I was very unhappy, I missed a lot of days—Mum didn't really make me go. Eventually when I moved out from my mum's to my dad's, I just never got back into it.

Jessica's case illustrates that drug use was one of a number of factors explaining her pathway out of school. Understanding her drug use within a social-ecological framework would ask us to identify the interconnections between factors such as her environment, economic position and social connections. Doing this helps us understand the interplay between a home life where there was housing instability and parental drug use, along with poor connection with community (school), combined with her mental health issues. Certainly Jessica stopped attending of her own volition, but there was also not anybody asking her why she was not at school.

Participants were quick to acknowledge that they were not the ideal student; nor that they especially enjoyed school. Some regretted not having an education, but most regretted leaving school because of what they ended up doing instead: very little, other than meeting up with mates, smoking bongs and hanging around. Despite disliking the structure of school, for many of these young people, the school bell ringing at set times each day was the only structure that they had in their lives. Leaving this behind left them with a sense of purposelessness and many hours to fill each day, with a very limited group of people.

The separation from school was a critical disconnection in their lives. For most, substance use had been a part of their lives before leaving school. But it was once they were out of school and left with hours of time to pass that drugs became a significant issue. This was exacerbated by the reality that most left school directly into unemployment.

Unemployment

Unstable living arrangements, and a growing drug problem, explain why so many of the participants left school early. These factors also partly explain why most of them became unemployed upon leaving school, although limited literacy and a poor educational record were contributing factors. For many, employment was not even considered. This was not because they were lazy, but because they suspected they were "unemployable". Poor literacy and numeracy, and often very poor computer skills, hamper their employability.

The relationship between intergenerational unemployment/underemployment and substance abuse is an accepted part of the social imaginary. The story follows that families go for generations "rorting" the system—though certainly not living a life those paying tax may wish to trade places for. Intergenerational poverty is a particularly stigmatised domain. MacDonald et al. (2014) went looking for families where there were three generations of people without work. The difficulty they had in finding such families saw them relax their criteria and yet still they faced difficulty finding families where there were two generations of long-term unemployed. They concluded that arguments about intergenerational worklessness were akin to zombies: no evidence to support their existence yet people's belief that they exist was impossible to kill.

Despite the efforts of social scientists, it seems impossible to penetrate the belief that the poor are poor because they choose not to work. Shildrick and MacDonald (2013) found that even the poor blamed the poor for their circumstance! It seems infeasible that this view will not be challenged in the next generation where the divide between the education level of the poor and the rest will be acute. Put simply: in applying for very basic work, how can someone who left education at 14 compete with a generation of people who have bachelor degrees?

Understanding unemployment is important because in areas where there are high unemployment rates, there can also be higher rates of other markers of disadvantage such as crime and poor educational outcomes (Tinsley 2013). If we fail to understand the connections between these factors, we may perpetuate the view that people are impoverished because of their own personal failings.

For Simon, once the daily structure of school was no longer a part of his life, there was little to do:

[I was] smoking heaps of pot. I don't really remember. It just took up heaps of time. The whole day would be gone and I wouldn't realise. Weeks would go by

and I wouldn't realise ... I was smoking more than my mates because all of my friends still went to school and after Year 9 they kind of stopped doing it—they got over it—but I kept going because I was at home all day and I had nothing to do so I just smoked.

Jakey regretted leaving school, but this was not how he felt at the time:

I thought back then that I was too slick, that I was too cool for everyone. I was like "Fuck this! I am going to get money". I thought I was too cool for school and now I look back and I was the biggest idiot ever. Looking back, I'd be at uni now, but I didn't want to "waste" my time at school.

This was a common binary: young people had been desperate to leave school, only to quickly regret doing so.

Luke enjoyed his first few months away from school, explaining that it "was really good. I didn't care—no work, no nothing. No teachers telling me what to do. I could live my own life". Within a short period of time this faded and he began to miss school:

But I did like it [school]. Just the feeling of going there. And I had a lot of friends—people did like me; I was a nice person. I miss them—even now. I still wish that I had stayed—really wish that I had stayed at school. That's the only reason that I feel that everything is happening and that I've gone downhill— 'cause I left school.

These young people were aware that their employment options were bleak. Not having completed secondary education was a barrier to future opportunities, given that they belonged to a generation where more than 80 per cent of young people will complete school (DEECD 2013). The proliferation of undergraduate university degrees leaves those without even a high school certification considerably disadvantaged. This was something which Alex was feeling:

Just looking at some of the kids, looking at other people's lives—kids I used to go to school with and the potential they have compared to me. Sometimes I feel like, "Fuck, I could be that person", but I have taken the wrong path.

Alex takes individual responsibility for taking the "wrong path". However, her decision to leave school was influenced by the fact there was no integration aide at her high school, as well as becoming homeless to escape sexual abuse. To infer that Alex had a free "choice" is simplistic. Nonetheless, Alex adopts complete agency in her narrative. This is consistent with the participants in Bourgois's (2002) landmark study of "crack" dealers in the USA. They rejected any suggestion that they were "victims of circumstance" and emphasised their own agency in choosing to become street-based crack dealers. This is like participants in this study who felt that their behaviour caused abuse, or their disinterest alone was why they were not at school. Similarly, MacDonald, who has undertaken extensive work on the "economically marginal" in the UK, points out that individuals in these areas experience public social issues as personal troubles (MacDonald 2008).

There was little reflection from the young people about their experiences of unemployment and I suspected this was because they found it boring—and therefore had little to say about it. There were a small number of young people who gained paid work, but this was often on a casual or part-time basis, and in most cases it did not last long, often because of housing instability. Most of these young people were on the outside of the labour market and it would take significant change in their life—particularly formal education—for them to be competitive in finding permanent full-time work. Simply "choosing" to want to work would not make them employable.

Homelessness

Homelessness is the most chronic marker of disadvantage. In Australia in 2014–15, specialist housing services were accessed by 41,780 young people (MacKenzie et al. 2016). Youth homelessness has been an issue of policy attention since the late 1980s with the release of the National Inquiry into youth homelessness, *Our Homeless Children*, more commonly referred to as "The Burdekin Report" (Burdekin 1989). This report led to the pilot of many early intervention and youth-specific services (Chamberlain and MacKenzie 1998). While many of these services have shown to be effective, the problem persists. Part of the reason for this is that youth homelessness is perhaps the most "downstream" a young person can be, perhaps only surpassed by institutionalisation. If homelessness is used as a point of intervention, then the intervention is coming too late. But how do we identify who is at risk of becoming homeless? Here the issue becomes clearer for what it is: a poverty issue. People who become homeless are in both economic and social poverty first. Family breakdown is often the tipping point for entry into homelessness, so by the time someone is homeless, that is one factor among many that need intensive support.

The vast majority of participants had experienced homelessness: 96 per cent of the women and 86 per cent of the men. Of the six participants who had not been homeless, only two had genuinely stable housing. These were Maggie and Michael, and my questions about stable housing seemed odd to them. For instance, when I asked Michael if he had ever been kicked out of home, he replied, "But *where* would I go!" The possibility that a parent would evict a son or daughter was unthinkable to him. Michael had been raised in a family where, despite many issues, children were to be cared for. This was also how Maggie felt. Michael's reply illustrated the sense of security that was missing in the other young people's lives.

Understanding young people's pathways into homelessness can help determine the supports they are likely to need. Toro et al. (2011) undertook a longitudinal study with 250 young people entering homelessness in Detroit. The researchers propose a three-category typology: (1) transient but connected, (2) high-risk, and (3) low-risk. The "transient but connected" group had the longest histories of homelessness, but the members of this group were the most connected to their families and had other social supports and networks. The members of the high-risk group were those most likely to have substance use and mental health issues, along with disconnection from their family. The low-risk group comprised people who presented with the lowest severity on each indicator. All of the participants in my study who had been homeless fell within the "high-risk category", although a minority were still connected with their families, which gives them more protective factors, in that there were people in their lives who, to some degree, cared about them.

Becoming Homeless

Entry into youth homelessness is diverse. Abuse, neglect and leaving the care system are all common features, with children leaving care having much higher rates of homelessness (Biehal and Wade 1999). As we saw earlier, 90 per cent of the young people had been homeless. Asiah came to Australia from Sudan as a child refugee without his parents. He lived with his older stepsister, though this arrangement soon became acrimonious and she kicked him out when he was 14. Asiah left school soon after this, passing time by smoking marijuana. He explained: "Smoking weed makes you forget everything."

Roxanne had a stable, albeit strict, family life. However, she had been raped, and soon after, both her best friend and her grandfather had died. One day she got drunk at school and was suspended. Her father was furious and threatened to kick her out of home, rather than motivate her to "straighten up". This left Roxanne feeling more alone:

> All those people had died. Every time I was at home I was getting yelled at and told that I was a worthless piece of shit. I didn't really have any steady friends.

Roxanne's drug use increased steadily, and true to his word, her father did kick her out of home. Roxanne spent many years feeling abandoned and unloved and she found that drug use softened this.

About three-quarters (72 per cent) of the young people became homeless at around the same time that they left school. It appeared that for the majority, the disconnection from school was the catalyst for the disconnection from home. Becoming homeless "locked" young people into unemployment and made a return to education virtually impossible. Many reported feeling isolated and depressed.

Luke was kicked out of his mother's home not long after he was expelled from school. He had "lost the plot", and his mother had an intervention order placed against him. Luke explained that his "losing the plot" was closely related to his heavy cannabis use. He said that he "couldn't handle" the drugs, which only exacerbated his depression. Luke went to live with his father, but this did not work out:

I wasn't happy living there. I don't know. I ended up leaving his house—it was just before I turned 15—I just left and then I wasn't at my mum's or my dad's.

Luke stayed temporarily with various friends and acquaintances. When he turned 16, he became eligible to receive a government welfare payment and was able to rent a room. Luke explained that this "wasn't too bad". After having been homeless for so long, it took little to impress Luke: "I got food, I had a roof over my head, I had a bed—I made it work." This arrangement ended when Luke was evicted.

The quick transition from family conflict to homelessness was also experienced by Sam, who was raised by a single father, but their relationship deteriorated during Sam's teenage years:

He kept telling me to get work, and then when I did get work, he was still complaining about stuff, and we just didn't really get along so I thought I'd leave but I ended up being on the streets.

Sam was on the streets for 18 months before he found a youth refuge. He was unaware that there were services able to provide support for him. By the time that he did, he was very disconnected from his former life.

Katte was another case where fleeing the home was more desirable than being there. As I probed how it was that her apparently caring—but "boring"—parents would let her remain homeless, it became clear that the ordinary, middle-class home life that Katte had portrayed was not entirely accurate. Katte went on to talk about feeling safer on the streets, "cause my dad used to hit me a lot". While Katte's own narrative about her homelessness had been framed with a sense of agency—she "chose" to run away from her "boring" family—the reality appeared to be that she was, in fact, fleeing ongoing physical abuse, and it was not just Katte's father who was violent. When Katte's mother discovered that Katte had a tattoo, she "went fucking crazy", slapping Katte before pushing her head into the bonnet of the car. Katte said that her family had a "nice home", but she would "rather be homeless than be with them".

Many of the young people appeared to have been escaping from their family home. Lisa's undisclosed abuse at her after-school care program had affected her in many ways. While the sexual abuse had not happened at home, there were other issues of family violence and neglect within the family. When I asked Lisa how she became homeless, she answered, "I went to the city with my friend and I ended up staying there for three years." In a literal sense, this was true, but Lisa was also escaping violence which impeded her ability to make a free choice to move out.

Some young people were abandoned by their caregivers. For example, Jai's entry to homelessness came at 14 when he "came out" as gay and his grandfather no longer wanted anything to do with him. As we saw earlier, this led to him engaging in sex work in order to gain shelter and basic provisions.

As we can see, pathways into homelessness were varied—and, not surprisingly, no one travelled exactly the same route—but one consistent consequence of becoming homeless was that most young people were now disconnected from family, home and school. Their new life of transience was a critical juncture in their pathway to substance abuse.

Being Homeless: "It Just Made You Feel Un-Homed"

Each explanation for how a young person became homeless was unique, but there were also common themes in their narratives. Many of the young people felt abandoned by one or both parents. In some cases this was literal and the young person was evicted. In other cases it was figurative when the parent abandoned the role of caregiver. Others had "homes" with a parent in them, but these homes were characterised by abuse and neglect. Many of the young people, particularly women, made reference to feeling safer on the streets. This tells us little about the streets but a lot about the severity of their home life.

Every participant had a clear memory of what happened when they became homeless, but their recollections of daily life after they became homeless were often quite hazy. They recalled dramatic events but not the more mundane aspects of their day-to-day lives. One thing that people did remember was that they often did not know how to get assistance with housing or food when they first became homeless.

Voni was transient for a long period of time. Sometimes she could not find anywhere to stay:

There were times when I got kicked out and had nowhere to go ... I didn't know where to go. I didn't know that if you were homeless there were actually places that you could go.

Ebony was also unaware of services for food or accommodation. The lack of services combined with her naivety did not bode well:

I slept at the bottom of a staircase and I had these really weird people looking at me. An old man kept watching me and I had to get changed there, I had to go to the toilet there—at the bottom of the stairs where I was sleeping ... It was really disgusting ... I was only 13 at the time.

Ebony began to access services only when she was 16—three years after becoming homeless. Ebony nonchalantly explained that after sleeping in the staircase, she decided, "I'll sell myself". However, she went to the main strip and saw the working girls and quickly realised that that was not something she could do. When I asked her what made her think of doing this, she said she had "no idea". I wondered whether the sexual abuse at the hands of her stepfather had taught her that women's bodies were a commodity that could be traded.

For those who lived on the streets, the experience was a sharp learning curve. According to Jahl:

Roaming the streets, not doing anything ... I just kicked it with all the younger kids that were in the city ... That was a fucking terrible part of my life. That's why I am mature today. I went there young and naïve, and I went through so much stupid stuff. Perverts, paedophiles, punch-ons—just bad people. I learned how to read people ... it was mostly [minor] dramas, but then there was also stuff that you're going to carry with you for life.

Participants often recalled the events of homelessness, but their narratives were told as a series of experiences, almost separate from the embodied, emotional aspect. I asked, "How did it *feel*?" to which Riley replied, "It was fucking scary. I'd walk until I couldn't walk anymore—literally—and I would just fall down on the road ... then I'd wake up later." Roxanne, who entered homelessness after her father kicked her out for being drunk at school, offered a detailed insight:

It's a different feeling when you are homeless. You don't even really feel like a person anymore. You just feel like a piece of garbage on the side of the street. That's how people view you and that's how you feel.

Roxanne illuminates how her embodied self felt disconnected from the social community in which she was living. The homeless are those most closely connected to our cities' spaces by virtue of the time they spend in them, yet these streets are lonely and isolate.

Asiah also described the desolation of homelessness:

You don't know where you're gonna go, what you're gonna do, where you're gonna eat, when you're gonna sleep … it kind of like freezes your mind … Sometimes you just do stuff or go places because you don't have anything to do … I started getting scared because there's nothing to do.

The challenges of homelessness were compounded by the reasons people were homeless. Asiah used drugs use to help him deal with his homelessness as well as the desolation he felt about leaving his family as a child. Asiah was trying to find comfort in a world where there was none.

The effects of homelessness on young people's emotional well-being were considerable though this finding is neither surprising nor new (see: Johnson and Chamberlain 2011; MacKenzie et al. 2016). Christina was succinct: "It was depressing, extremely depressing. It just makes you feel un-homed—like you don't fit in anywhere." The feelings of despair that Christina expressed, combined with the ready availability of drugs, made substance use an attractive option for "killing pain".

Once on the street, the availability of drugs increased significantly. Ashly, who was sleeping on the streets, lived in a world filled with violence and drug use:

It was everywhere—people robbing. That was when the heroin season started getting really bad. I just used to follow my sister. She was 14 at the time … and I just used to follow her around everywhere because she was the one with the heroin. I was scared. I hated the stuff, I hated the people, so I just used to follow her everywhere they went and just watch them. I'd go up alleyways and watch them, and help them if they're going off their heads. They tried to tell me to piss off, you know, "You're just a little girl", but I was like, "I'm not going around the corner in case you drop dead".

Despite all of this, Ashly did not start using drugs herself—she was determined not to. As we saw earlier, her drug use came a few years later.

There is no clear pattern as to the relationship between homelessness and substance abuse. In a study of 4291 homeless people, Johnson and Chamberlain (2008b) found that 43 per cent had substance abuse issues, but two-thirds of them developed their substance abuse issue after becoming homeless. It was certainly the case for the young people in the current study that homelessness made drugs both more available and more appealing.

Voni began using before she was kicked out of home, but homelessness brought a sharp increase in her use:

> *Even just when it was cold, I'd want to have a hit to numb me out and not think of anything. Yeah, definitely more using.*

Voni used heroin for the first time after being raped—heroin worked well for anaesthetising her emotions. Her heroin use led to her becoming homeless, and being homeless was far more bearable if she was stoned, so her heroin use increased. Emotional and psychological distress was experienced by all of the young people in this study, and drug use helped them manage these symptoms—but drug use was not a foolproof solution.

Eleven (44 per cent) of the young women disclosed a suicide attempt as did six (17 per cent) of the young men, an overall rate of 28 per cent. Riley had tried to hang herself in a boarding house, which is an unusual method for a woman (Canetto and Sakinofsky 1998; Denning et al. 2000). She was found unconscious by a member of cleaning staff and was revived.

Jazmine had attempted suicide three times. She recalls her experience in a hospital emergency department:

> *They made me feel so small that I didn't want to have anything to do with their services at all … I remember that two people came in … and they just said, "Are you Jazmine?" … then they were like, "What have you gone and done to yourself now? … So what are we going to do with you? This is the third time now, we can't let this keep happening", and they just preached at me like that.*

This response left Jazmine feeling dejected and more isolated.

Suicide was a topic that was unearthed later in the interview, after childhood and adolescence had been canvassed. Almost invariably, suicide attempts came in the period after disconnection from family, home and school. When participants spoke about their suicide attempts, their desperation was clear: they did not want to die but could not bear to live.

Alternative Pathway

There were six young people in the sample who had never been homeless, though their trajectories into substance abuse were not a case of "bad luck". Three of them used drugs to help mask mental health symptoms and I will examine them in the next section. The other three I will examine now.

One of them was Gerald, who came from a background that was typical of many of the participants. He was raised in a home where there was abuse, neglect and very heavy parental drug use. Gerald's stepfather would often end up in violent rages after drinking alcohol. As a consequence, Gerald hated alcohol because he associated it with his stepfather's violence. Nonetheless, his introduction to alcohol came early:

> *I was about nine or ten. My stepfather bought me some Wild Turkey [Bourbon] and taught me to be a man. I got really drunk and then he made me bounce on the trampoline. That day really hurt, I felt really, really sick.*

Like the other young people who grew up in families where drug use was normal, Gerald followed in his stepfather's footsteps.

The other two young men, Michael and Jakey, were both atypical of the broader sample. Both had a father who had had an affair, and both had a younger sister who was "devastated" as a consequence. After their father's infidelity, Michael and Jakey were left deeply troubled about what it meant to "be a man". The link between their emotional trauma and substance abuse is explored in greater detail in Chap. 6.

Mental Health

In total, 53 of the 61 (87 per cent) young people had a mental health issue and there was no significant difference between men and women (men: 86 per cent; women: 88 per cent). The most common diagnoses for both genders were anxiety, depression and psychosis. There were six young people whose primary mental health diagnosis was likely to be organic: these are the psychiatric disorders which are believed to have strong biological and genetic foundations such as schizophrenia and bipolar disorder.

There were 47 young people whose mental health issues were not inherently biological or genetic. Their diagnoses were mostly depression, anxiety and psychosis. It is almost certain that environmental factors were impacting on the mental health of these 47 young people, although separating organic factors from lifestyle factors is impossible.

There were three young people in the sample who had not been homeless but who had developed a problem with substance abuse in the process of self-medicating to manage their mental health symptoms. They were Larry, Andreas and Maggie.

The two men, Larry and Andreas, came from stable families, where both parents remained together. Andreas had thoroughly enjoyed primary school and the early years of high school where he won academic awards. However, by Year 9, things had come unstuck:

I got diagnosed with psychosis, schizophrenia, depression—all that sort of stuff.

Soon after this, Andreas started to experiment with drugs which stopped the voices he was hearing. However, this cessation of symptoms was only temporary. Later, he found that drugs sometimes made his symptoms worse:

As soon as I had the bongs I knew it was a psychotic episode. I started hallucinating, seeing things, and it got real bad. There were people screaming in my head, full screaming. Then what happened was, I was trying to walk home but I realised that I was just stepping up and down, I wasn't walking, and I was like, punching trees, all this shit. I went to the station, and I had a knife, and

> *I thought someone was fighting me, so I stabbed them. And then I just lost my shit, and the next day was the first mental health appointment, and I got there and I told them what was happening and they knew straight away.*

While Andreas knew that drugs were "bad" for him, he also knew that they had been able to give him relief from some of the symptoms which his prescribed medication appeared unable to manage. In a similar vein, Larry had experienced psychosis long before he was formally diagnosed and medicated for a psychotic disorder. By chance he had discovered that the cannabis his friends were smoking socially helped to mask the thoughts and voices that were intruding in on his head.

Maggie also came from a stable family environment and had a childhood free from abuse or neglect. However, her mental health issues were significant. Maggie was bright, warm and had a loving family, but her obsessive-compulsive disorder and her depression severely limited her potential. There were days when she could not get out of bed. Her anxiety crippled her and she found that cannabis helped control these symptoms:

> *It relaxes me, it slows me down. It slowed all my thought processes down. It puts things in order in my head and it clarifies a whole lot of things so that I can just see one thing at a time—the first thing that I need to do, and then the second thing. And I can check boxes and check things off, 'cause I like checking boxes.*

After one stay in a psychiatric hospital, she was prescribed a new medication. At first, this appeared to work well:

> *I just bounced into life. I was so happy. I was like, "I'm in recovery!" I was off dope ... I was doing really well ... and then I just crashed again. I was like, "I can't deal with this anxiety" ... so I saw my psychiatrist and I basically said to him, "I can't deal with this anxiety, I can't deal with hour long panic attacks every night".*

Maggie knew that cannabis was able to calm her, and soon enough, she relapsed into substance abuse as a way of stopping the panic attacks.

Conclusion

In Chap. 3, we saw that my participants had many problems in their childhoods, but these were not drug problems. This chapter has examined what happened in their adolescent years that led to substance abuse problems. For the majority, secondary school was a largely unhappy experience, with only seven (12 per cent) completing Year 12, compared with 80 per cent of their age group.

Most had begun to try alcohol and other drugs while they were still at school, although it was not their substance abuse which had led to their departure. Housing instability, family breakdown and developmental issues had all created barriers that made staying at school a difficult option. Half (53 per cent) of the young women did not complete Year 10, nor did two-thirds (66 per cent) of the young men, and most of the remainder left school at the end of Year 10 or early in Year 11.

The separation from school was a critical disconnection in their lives. Most had been recreational drug users since their early teens, but once they were out of school, drugs became a significant issue. This was exacerbated by the reality that most left school directly into unemployment. Substance abuse was an effective way of "killing time", especially so for those who were without housing.

The vast majority (90 per cent) of participants had experienced homelessness, and in many cases this occurred roughly around the time they left school. If substance abuse had not been an issue prior to homelessness, it quickly became one once they engaged with other homeless people. This chapter has shown that there was not a single pathway from childhood trauma to substance abuse, but there were key factors—leaving school, separation from family, unemployment and homelessness—that were usually "in the mix".

Thus far, I have described the experiences of the young people in this study. But what do we make of this? It is not helpful to conclude that childhood trauma and poverty led to their substance abuse as though it is a causal phenomenon: plenty of traumatised poor people get by without a drug problem. However, it is well established that those who experience problematic drug use have higher incidences of early-life trauma and disadvantage. So it is necessary to undertake a richer analysis of this. Some level of correlation is clear: but how does childhood trauma manifest as a drug problem for some? The chapters that follow seek to dig "below the surface" to answer this question. First, we see that there are gender differences. In turn, we examine the young women first before turning our attention to the young men. Various theories are used to help explain the complex interaction of phenomena at play.

References

Biehal, N., & Wade, J. (1999). I thought it would be easier: The early housing careers of young people leaving care. In J. Rugg (Ed.), *Young people, housing and social policy* (pp. 79–92). London, UK: Routledge.

Bourgois, P. (2002). *In search of respect: Selling crack in El Barrio* (2nd ed.). New York: Cambridge University Press, (e-book).

Burdekin, B. (1989). *Our homeless children : Report of the national inquiry into homeless children.* Canberra, Australia: Human Rights and Equal Opportunity Commission, Australian Government Publishing Service.

Canetto, S. S., & Sakinofsky, I. (1998). The gender paradox in suicide. *Suicide and Life-Threatening Behavior, 28*(1), 1–23.

Chamberlain, C., & MacKenzie, D. (1998). *Youth homelessness: Early intervention and prevention.* Sydney, Australia: Australian Centre for Equity through Education.

Denning, D. G., Conwell, Y., King, D., & Cox, C. (2000). Method choice, intent, and gender in completed suicide. *Suicide and Life-Threatening Behavior, 30*(3), 282–288.

Department of Education and Early Childhood Development (DEECD). (2013). Victorian child and adolescent monitoring system—14.4 age of initiation of young people in drug use. Retrieved February 26, 2014, from http://www.education.vic.gov.au/about/research/pages/144ageofdruguse.aspx

Elliott, D., Huizinga, D., & Menard, S. (1989). *Multiple problem youth: Delinquency, substance use and mental health problems.* New York: Springer.

Johnson, G., & Chamberlain, C. (2008a). From youth to adult homelessness. *Australian Journal of Social Issues, 43*(4), 563–582.

Johnson, G., & Chamberlain, C. (2008b). Homelessness and substance abuse: Which comes first? *Australian Social Work, 61*(4), 342–356.

Johnson, G., & Chamberlain, C. (2011). Are the homeless mentally ill? *Australian Journal of Social Issues, 46*(1), 29–48.

MacDonald, R. (2008). Disconnected youth? Social exclusion, the "underclass" & economic marginality. *Social Work & Society, 6*(2), 236–248.

MacDonald, R., Shildrick, T., & Furlong, A. (2014). In search of "intergenerational cultures of worklessness": Hunting the Yeti and shooting zombies. *Critical Social Policy, 34*(2), 199–220.

MacKenzie, D., Flatau, P., Steen, A., & Thielking, M. (2016). *The cost of youth homelessness in Australia.* Research Briefing. Retrieved April 29, 2016, from http://apo.org.au/files/Resource/d_mackenzie_cost_of_youth_homelessness_full_report_2016.pdf

Newburn, T., & Shiner, M. (2005). *Dealing with disaffection: Young people, mentoring and social inclusion.* Portland, OR: Willan Publishing.

Shildrick, T., & MacDonald, R. (2013). Poverty talk: How people experiencing poverty deny their poverty and why they blame "the poor". *The Sociological Review, 61*(2), 285–303.

Tinsley, M. (2013). *Cultures of dependency: Fact, fiction, solution.* London: Policy Exchange.

Toro, P. A., Lesperance, T. M., & Braciszewski, J. M. (2011). *The heterogeneity of homeless youth in America: Examining typologies.* Homelessness Research Institute. Retrieved June 28, 2014, from http://www.onefamilyinc.org/Blog/wp-content/uploads/2011/10/homeless_youth_in_america.pdf

5

Cutting Out the Pain: Sexual Abuse, Self-Injury, Abandonment and Young Women's Substance Abuse

Early on in the data collection I began to suspect that there were gender differences in explaining pathways into problematic substance use. Of the first six women interviewed, five had shared similar life experiences, and strikingly, the young women all used the same language to describe these experiences. One of the issues that came up repeatedly was that when these women were younger they had engaged in self-injurious behaviour—"cutting". Often people are reluctant to disclose this behaviour, because they are aware that in the wider society, cutting is stigmatised and carries connotations of pathology.

I had not planned to ask any questions about self-injury. However, if young people raised the issue themselves, I would offer them a space to talk about their experiences. By asking these questions in a non-judgmental fashion, it indicated to the participants that I cared to know what they were talking about. The stories that came from these young women were very confronting, and the gender differences also highlight the utility in undertaking a feminist analysis of this issue in future work. For now though, the focus is on understanding, through a symbolic interactionist perspective, what their experiences were.

© The Author(s) 2016
K. Daley, *Youth and Substance Abuse,*
DOI 10.1007/978-3-319-33675-6_5

Twenty (77 per cent) out of the 26 young women disclosed that they had engaged in cutting when they were in primary school or in their early teens. We already know that unemployment and homelessness have some connection with substance abuse; it was now apparent that self-injury was a common factor too. Now I want to examine this more closely and ask what the link is between self-injury and substance abuse.

First, I define self-injury, and I review two broad approaches to explain this activity. Then the chapter explores the childhood experiences of the 20 young women who had a history of cutting. It points out that all of them had experienced either sexual and/or emotional abuse. Focus then turns to the phenomenon of "dissociation". This is a psychological defence mechanism that helps people cope with abuse by separating the mind from the body. Finally, the chapter shows that self-injury and substance abuse served a similar purpose for these young women: they were different ways of "cutting out the pain".

Self-Injury

Definition and Social Characteristics

Self-injury refers to the purposeful, non-suicidal injury of oneself. The most common form of self-injury is cutting. Other types include burning, bruising, pinching or wound interference. The severity of self-injury varies. It is often mild with superficial wounds not requiring medical treatment, but it can sometimes be so severe that it is life-threatening (Adler and Adler 2011; Levenkron 1998). Self-injury is sometimes referred to as "self-harm" or "self-mutilation", and both the terms imply that self-injury is irrational behaviour that is damaging to a person's physical well-being. In the wider community, self-injury carries connotations of mental illness. It is taken for granted that self-injury is a deeply stigmatised form of behaviour and that those who self-injure should not disclose their "deviance" to other people.

Self-injury is associated with women. However, little is known about the demographic characteristics of the self-injuring population. It is difficult to assess the representativeness of various research samples.

Studies drawn from psychiatrists' case studies portray the typical "cutter" as a middle-class white schoolgirl (Favazza 1996; Levenkron 1998). Similarly, Strong's (1998) book on the topic reported that people who self-injure are usually women, although many of those who were interviewed for this research were well past their teens. Chandler (2012b) interviewed 12 people aged 12–37 years and purposively sampled to include both men and women (7 females, 5 males). Adler and Adler (2011) undertook 135 in-depth interviews with people who had self-injured. They reported that 85 per cent of their sample were females. Likewise, Presson and Rambo (2016) had 9 women in a sample of 12 who had previously self-injured.

In Australia, Martin et al. (2010) completed a cross-sectional telephone survey of 12,006 people drawn from a representative sample of the adult population. They found that self-injury was most common in the age group 20–24 and that 24 per cent of young women aged 20–24 had self-injured, compared with 18 per cent of men. In the USA, Tyler et al. (2003) examined the prevalence of self-injury in a sample of 428 homeless teenagers. They found that 69 per cent had at least one episode of self-injury, though there was no significant difference between males and females. Overall, there is considerable uncertainty about the characteristics of people who self-injure. Reliable statistics are almost impossible to obtain because most people who self-injure conceal their activities and there are sampling biases with almost all studies undertaken thus far.

Two Explanatory Frameworks

There are two broad approaches to explaining self-injury. The first approach views self-injury as evidence of pathology. I refer to this as the "common sense explanation". The second approach views self-injury as a form of "coping" behaviour that must be understood in context. According to this approach, self-injury may be "unconventional" but is not "pathological" (Alexander and Clare 2004; Crouch and Wright 2004; Harris 2000). There are a number of versions of this argument. I refer to them as "contextual explanations".

The common sense explanation rests on the assumption that the intentional injury of oneself is extremely disconcerting. This discomfort is generally exacerbated when the injury involves perforating one's flesh. The sight of blood is confronting as the breaking of the body's boundaries is a powerful symbolic gesture which is deeply embedded within the social imaginary as something deviant and/or pathological. Hodgson (2004) has suggested that attempts to classify self-injury as a form of mental illness is a consequence of society's need to explain that which appears "irrational" or "pathological".

In fact, self-injury is a feature of several formal psychiatric diagnoses. However, in the recently released fifth edition of the *Diagnostic and Statistical Manual of Mental Disorders*, "non-suicidal self-injury" was listed as "section three" disorders. These are disorders which may not be covered by health insurance in the USA and that "require further research" (American Psychiatric Association 2013). Prior to non-suicidal self-injury having its own diagnostic criteria, these injuries were seen as pathological forms of behaviour and thought to be closely associated with borderline personality disorders (Cameron et al. 2012; NIMH n.d.).

The common-sense approach to self-injury assumes there is something inherently wrong with this behaviour and is consistent with the heavy psychiatric lens through which self-injury has often been viewed by medical professionals (Adler and Adler 2011; Chandler et al. 2011; Hodgson 2004). Psychiatrist Armando Favazza (1996) has written extensively on self-injury. He calls for a different approach from mainstream psychiatry. He refers to his approach as "cultural psychiatry". Cultural psychiatry adopts a more holistic understanding of people's psychopathologies by assessing the role and place of culture in their lives. Nonetheless, cultural psychiatry still views individuals as "patients" and cutting as a symptom of pathology.

There is a small body of sociological work which questions the assumption that self-injury is indicative of psychopathology. These studies suggest that self-injury may actually be meaningful behaviour if it is understood in context (Claes and Vandereycken 2007; Chandler 2012a). These "contextual explanations" come in a number of different forms.

Harris (2000) undertook a "correspondence study" where she exchanged letters with women who self-injured to learn about the contexts in which they cut themselves and found that there was a "situated logic" to young women's cutting. Many of her participants explained that the intention of their self-injury was to "cut out the bad". Rather than focusing on the "bad" being intrinsic to the individual, Harris was curious to understand how the "bad" ever "got in". She began from the viewpoint that the negative emotions which instigated self-injury were not manifestations of an individual's pathology but a consequence of an individual's experiences.

Harris (2000) suggests that the oft-held view that self-injury is irrational is a consequence of Western society's privileging of dispassionate knowledge. When looking at self-injury in isolation from the individual's experience, the logic of the behaviour is impossible to see. This apparent absence has helped to reinforce the view that self-injury is a psychiatric issue. However, seeking to separate emotions and experiences from understandings of an inherently embodied phenomenon such as self-injury fails to capture a complete understanding of the function it serves for the person who engages in it (Chandler 2012a; Harris 2000; Horne and Csipke 2009).

There is some link between self-injury and substance abuse, although how strong the correlation is varies between studies. Klonsky and Moyer (2008) undertook a meta-analysis of the existing studies to establish the strength of the correlation and concluded that while there is a link, it is quite small and higher figures reported in individual studies are likely owing to population bias. It is complicated to establish, as many studies on self-injury recruit either participants or patient records from service providers, which leads to an over-representation of women with mental health issues and no real knowledge about the nature of the population of those who self-injure. However, within subpopulations such as females accessing mental health or substance abuse services, there may be a higher correlation between childhood sexual abuse and later self-injurious behaviour.

Strong (1998) suggests three possible explanations for the link between sexual abuse and self-injury. She argues that women who have been sexually abused experience extreme emotional pain, which often leads to separation of the mind from the body. They no longer identify with their own body and feel emotionally disconnected from their physical selves. Strong's first explanation for self-injury is that it disrupts these feelings of "dissociation" or emotional disconnectedness. Her second explanation is that it allows women to re-assert control over their bodies, which is taken away when they are raped. Her third explanation is women internalise intense emotional pain following rape, and self-injury symbolises "cutting out" the pain.

Other sociologists have focused on self-injury as a strategy for dealing with intense emotional pain and have drawn attention to the possibility that self-injury is a coping strategy. For example, Hodgson (2004) conducted an exploratory study which sought to understand how cutting is learned, as well as how people who cut manage the stigma with which it is associated. Adler and Adler (2011) undertook a major longitudinal study which drew attention to these issues, and I draw upon their study throughout this chapter. Similarly, Chandler's small empirical studies (2012a, 2012b) sought to extend the sociological literature and give voice to those who self-injure and who are not involved in psychiatric care.

Sociological studies draw attention to the social context in which people undertake self-injury and raise the possibility that self-injury is primarily a strategy for coping with intense emotional pain, although most analyses of self-injury have come from psychology. In the next two sections, I investigate the utility of a psychosocial approach. First, I examine the "social context" in which these young women grew up.

Childhood Trauma: The Body's Boundaries

There were 20 young women in this study who had a history of cutting. Of the 20, 16 (80 per cent) disclosed that they had been sexually abused as children and 14 (70 per cent) reported feeling "abandoned". This section explores these young women's early lives and their experiences of trauma.

Sexual Abuse

The topic of sexual abuse presented itself in a variety of ways within the participants' broader narratives. My background as a clinician informed these judgments, as did my understanding of Noddings's (2003) theory of relational ethics, which suggests that caring for people, and ensuring they feel cared for, should guide ethical reasoning. With care, I listened as these young women spoke, often tearfully. I do not offer comments on the highly emotive nature of the excerpts that follow. This is not because I am seeing to de-personalise them but that I feel that they speak for themselves—there is no need to point out that what has been said is sad.

Ebony had a biography that was typical among participants. When I asked her if as a teenager she had stayed at home much, she revealed:

Nup, never. I just ... I'd rather live at my friends' houses ... [where] I'd never get bashed or hurt in other ways. I'd always try to prevent going to my parents.

KD: Was there abuse at home?

Yeah, yeah. I got, er, ah ... by my so-called stepdad ... I was staying there, in the living room, in the fold-down bed, and he raped me. I was only 15 ... He bashed our family ... Yeah, we've bled a lot over him.

Lisa was also sexually abused. She was raised in a home of family violence and neglectful parenting, but her case differs from Ebony's in that her mother did not know about the sexual abuse and the perpetrator was not a family member. Lisa had spent three years sleeping on the streets in her early teenage years, and when asked if her safety had ever been compromised during this time, she explained that it had not been while she was on the streets, but it had earlier:

When I was in primary school, Dad wasn't there, because Mum had to go ... what it feels for me ... I am just trying to get the words—I am not very good with words, sorry ...

KD: No, take your time ...

... what made me, when I first was young, what started everything, being angry and sort of wanting to, I don't know, knick off somewhere or just drink, was because ... it was when Mum put me in after-school care and like, I feel that's what caused me to go off the rails a bit. Because, like, what happened ... it was one of the ladies' sons or something ... I couldn't tell my mum what he was doing, because, well [*starts crying*], I felt like I was going to get in trouble or something. Yeah, he just kept ... I had to go there every day. Mum sent me. Mum asked him to babysit me ... he just kept making me do shit with him [*sobbing*] ... I can still remember it.

Riley had also been sexually abused. For her, it was in the place she had sought refuge:

> *I was in Year 8 … it was one of my friends who I was staying with when my mum kicked me out—her dad sexually assaulted me. He always sexually assaulted my other friends when they stayed over too.*

Not long after this, Riley had moved interstate to a boarding school which an estranged—albeit caring—extended family member financed. However, this did not work out and she left. At one point, Riley was able to find accommodation in a share house and she attempted to return to a local public school for Year 11. However, with the complexities in her life this was not sustainable. Throughout all of this, there was no contact with her mother. When I asked if she missed her mother, Riley replied, "She really hurt me. She really, really hurt me." Riley did not admit that she missed her mother, yet she did not deny it either. Her pain was still raw and it was clear that she could not reconcile why she might miss someone who had hurt her so much. The young women often had many unresolved issues and were attempting to "move on" from these while simultaneously trying to build a new future.

Abandonment

Sexual abuse was not the only trauma that these young women experienced. Other traumatic events included parental mental illness and/or substance abuse, disconnection from school, housing instability, family violence and involvement in the child protection system. However, the most common trauma after sexual abuse was their sense of being abandoned. This affected 14 (70 per cent) of the young women. For the purposes of this chapter, abandonment refers to a young woman's ejection from the family home by her mother. I define "abandonment" in this way because most of these young women's biological fathers were not present in their lives.

Ebony's mother kicked her out of home when she was 13: "Mum sent me up to Melbourne, she just didn't want me anymore." When asked how that made her feel, she replied, "I cry, I cry every day. Every day I cry." Ebony's sadness about being kicked out was compounded by the reasons she was excluded from the family. Ebony's stepfather had been sexually abusing her and she felt that her mother was envious that her daughter was receiving his sexual attention:

Yeah, she knew [about the abuse], but she loved him. I'd ask her, "If you put us first, why didn't you leave him?", and she'd say, "I didn't have anywhere else to go", and I'd say, "Well, going anywhere is better than going back there", and she goes, "Yeah, well, I loved him and I didn't want to break his heart" ... I asked her again down the track, and she said, "When you've been with someone, you just become attached and you know, the sex just becomes, well, you know, you just really love it and you need it." That just really hurt me.

Lisa was aware that her mother did not know of her years of abuse at the after-school care programme, but she still felt a deep sense of hurt and abandonment that her mother had left her in this programme to be "cared" for. Later, Lisa's feeling of betrayal was cemented when she was literally abandoned:

One night my mum kicked me out basically, and I went down to my best friend's house, and into the city ... we both went into the city on a train and ended up staying in this squat with these old guys ... sometimes I would go back home, because they'd put a warrant out or something, and then I would go back and stay a couple of nights and we would have a fight or something and I would just go again. So yeah, I don't know, she got a bit sick of me being, just [a bit sick of] having a daughter, I guess.

In addition to this abandonment, there were other issues in Lisa's past which made living at home untenable. Lisa's stepfather was abusive, an issue not addressed by her mother. As Lisa shared this, her voice both lowered in volume and began to tremble in tone. The pain associated with this trauma was still raw. It was apparent that her mother's inaction caused just as much—if not more—distress than the assault itself. The absence of her mother's protection affected her not only physically but also psychologically as she felt that she had been neglected by the person who should have kept her safe.

A feeling of abandonment was echoed by Riley:

I was always having problems with Mum ever since I was a little kid. Always the little things: I was sporty, but she wanted me to do music. It was always a lot of hate with each other. Even though I was only so small … it got to the point where she just didn't want me anymore.

Pining for a mother's love was a common narrative. Lisa spent some time in the care of the state, an experience which she found mostly positive because it was the one place where she had both food and safety. Nonetheless, she eloquently captured the feeling of being without a parent's love: "If you don't have the affection from a parent and everything like that, you are an outcast in the world."

For 16-year-old Jessica, a volatile and problematic home environment increased the insurmountable pain she experienced after being abandoned:

She kicked me out and told me that us kids stole the best years of her life and she wished she never had us, that we were all spoilt little brats …
KD: Do you miss Mum?
Yes. I hate her so much that sometimes I think I could actually kill her, but … [*starts crying*] … she doesn't deserve fucking anything. She's an arsehole and that's the truth.

Jessica, like all of these young women, experienced a tension between feeling hurt and angry at her mother and a desperate want for her mother's love. We can see that these young women's trauma was not confined to their experiences of sexual abuse. The abuse the young women in this study experienced was compounded by the absence of support and safety. Often their mothers ignored or dismissed their cries for help and, not uncommonly, abandoned them entirely.[1]

---

[1] This is not to suggest that their mothers are entirely to blame or that the abandonment was a consequence of their mother's poor parenting. Often their mothers had also been raised in state care, and their poor parenting can only be blamed as much as the father's often absence. But the family is based at the very individual level and to understand how these young women were seemingly so frequently abandoned, it is necessary to understand the nature of intergenerational poverty and disadvantage.

Of the 20 young women who had self-injured, 16 had experienced sexual abuse and 14 had been abandoned (11 having experienced both). Only one young woman had experienced neither. Others have found strong relationships between self-injury and sexual abuse (Presson and Rambo 2016; Strong 1998), but still others have also suggested the relationship is due to sampling bias (Klonsky and Moyer 2008).

This section has explored these women's early lives and their experiences of trauma, paying particular attention to sexual abuse and abandonment. The young women did not have the support of their immediate or extended families. Rather than be nurtured, they were often trying to survive. In the next section, we see that the intense emotional pain that these women experienced, combined with a lack of physical safety, contributed to many of them having overwhelming feelings of dissociation.

Dissociation and Self-Injury

What Is Dissociation?

A woman's relationship with her body after sexual assault can be highly troubled as her sense of embodiment is violated. Adler and Adler (2011) argue that when women are very young they learn that their body is a commodity. After rape, many women are traumatised and some start to see their body as the "enemy" or the "cause" of their emotional agony.

It is also possible that some victims view their body as "seductress" and they blamed their bodies for attracting unwanted attention (as is so often the case in mainstream conjecture about whether "she asked for it"). Strong (1998) explains the relationship between sexual abuse and one's sense of embodiment:

> *Sexual abuse is the most obvious, and perhaps the most devastating, attack on body image. The body is never wholly one's own again. In fact, the victim's own body is used as a weapon against her. It is controlled by others and can be made to respond—the ultimate betrayal—against the owner's will. Its boundaries are violated and intruded upon, creating a lingering confusion between inner and outer ... An abused child may come to feel totally divorced from her physical self. (p. 122)*

After rape, the body can be seen as the enemy. Yet the body, the site of the trauma, is physically inescapable.

One strategy that women have for dealing with the trauma caused by rape is to "separate their mind from their body". In everyday language, we might say that they experience acute emotional numbness. Psychologists refer to this "separation of mind and body" as dissociation:

> *Dissociation in its more serious forms is a psychological defense mechanism that keeps traumatic memories, sensations, and feelings out of conscious awareness. It is a key defense used by abused children. In the face of overwhelming danger from which there is no physical escape, it is an ingenious bit of mental gymnastics ... **Mind and body separate. Pain is anaesthetized. The individual feels depersonalized: numb, unreal, outside oneself, a dispassionate observer rather than an anguished participant ... She can't remove her body from danger, but she can leave it emotionally.*** (Strong 1998, p. 38, emphasis added)

Dissociation is a strategy for the mind to help cope with stress by internalising emotional pain. When people experience very stressful situations, some individuals externalise the pain whereas others internalise it. Those who externalise emotional pain are likely to demonstrate their anger in ways that are immediate, obvious and visible: for example, yelling, screaming, swearing, punching a wall or vociferously blaming others.

In contrast, people who internalise their stress remain silent: they may bitterly reflect on their disappointment; become intensely angry with themselves; or become moody, withdrawn and resentful; but always remain silent, internalising their pain, not speaking out. Disassociation is a strategy for dealing with emotional pain and internalised stress. Women who have been sexually abused often internalise their emotional pain because they feel that they cannot talk about what has happened. To reveal that one has been sexually abused is to run the risk that they themselves can be perceived as having put "oneself at risk" or having been "complicit in the encounter". We are all familiar with the cruel assertion that "she probably asked for it".

Women who have been raped often experience dissociation. They may start to see their body as "the enemy" or to blame their body for attracting unwanted attention, yet their own body is their physical prison. Dissociation involves separating the psychological self from the physical self and it brings with it its own problems. Shutting off the mind from the body led many of the young women in the current study to say that they no longer felt alive. The dissociation had left them feeling numb.

At the same time, internalising their emotional pain meant that they had not been able to rid themselves of the destructive emotions that accompany rape. For some, this meant they had internalised a deep sense of self-loathing, for their body was perceived as the impetus for their troubles.

Feeling Alive and Cutting Out the Pain

There are three explanations for the link between sexual abuse and cutting. The first I will call *disrupting dissociation.* Strong (1998) points out that the visibility of the blood disrupts the young woman's dissociated state and provides evidence that despite their emotional numbness, they are in fact alive. Horne and Csipke (2009) also say that cutting can be used to suspend an intolerable emotional state, to disrupt dissociation (see also: Suyemoto 1998). In that, the perforation of the skin and sight of the blood shocks the woman back to an embodied sense of self.

This explanation aligned well with several participants in this study. When asked what she liked about self-injury, Stevie replied: "It made me feel like I was alive." In fact, when asked about the function or purpose of self-injury, the descriptive language participants adopted was profoundly similar. The frequency in which "feeling alive" was used to describe self-injury was what initially alerted me to it being a common phenomenological pattern among participants. Lizzie also explained, "I just felt like I deserved it ... so that I knew that I was alive," as did Katte, who stated that "[i]t was the only thing that made me feel alive." To need to do something to feel "alive" implied that they were previously feeling in a way which was not alive, not dead, but numb, which is consistent with the previous discussion of dissociation.

A second explanation for the link between cutting and sexual abuse is that cutting symbolically releases the emotional pain that is internalised within the body when dissociation takes place. I will refer to this as *cutting out the pain*. This implies that the neat conceptual understanding that the woman who has experienced dissociation cuts herself to feel alive is not an adequate account on its own. This explanation argues that there is, in fact, a more complex relationship between self-injury and dissociation. Suyemoto (1998) accepts that one purpose of self-injury is to disrupt dissociation, enabling people to feel "alive", but she also suggests that for some women, the purpose is to cut out emotional pain that has been internalised as a consequence of dissociation. Adler and Adler (2011) also reported that both motivations were present among the participants in their study.

The need to release overwhelming emotions was cited consistently among the young women in this study. The sight of blood itself seemed to be therapeutic in that it was a symbolic release of these emotions. When asked what she liked about self-injury, Alex replied:

> I don't know. It was like a release. After I'd seen the blood, it was like a release of anger or some sort of release. I can't really explain the feeling, but it was just a release.

"Releasing" pain in a controlled way, where the woman feels as though she is in command of her body, is a theme found by others (Chandler 2012b; Harris 2000; Horne and Csipke 2009). Alex's feelings were similar to those expressed by Riley, whose deep sense of self-loathing and overflow of heavy emotions were the catalyst for her self-injury:

> I'd hate myself so much, and I'd just feel so much pain, and just feeling … I don't know how to put it … just seeing myself hurting, I don't know … It's because you hate yourself. You hate yourself. I don't know—seeing the pain when I did it—it helped.

Riley's description of "*seeing* the pain", as opposed to "*feeling* the pain", illuminates that for these young women, the pain associated with self-injury was emotional rather than physical. Chandler (2012a, 2012b) has discussed how society's privileging of physical pain over emotional pain is a consistent theme among people who self-injure. People use self-injury as a way of turning emotional pain into physical pain because physical pain is seen as more valid. Harris (2000), as well as Horne and Csipke (2009), also found this a common pattern among their respective participants.

Emotional anguish was pervasive among my participants. Stevie was engulfed with a deep sense of sadness. Self-injury helped her to "feel things other than hate and negativity and depression". The search for emotions other than depression was common. Mary, for instance, pointed out, "It's the only thing that makes you feel some other way than what you are feeling." For these women, self-injury was "cutting out the pain". Although this may initially seem a bizarre way of dealing with emotions, Amanda, a participant in Hodgson's (2004) study into self-injury, points out that it may not be as unusual as it first appears:

> *Cutting, even at 11, is not REALLY such a foreign idea. We cut the brown part off our apple when we eat it, we cut the dead leaves off house plants, we cut the grass when it no longer looks neat and tidy, heck, we even cut out body parts when they no longer work right. Even small children want you to cut the part they don't like off [like the crust off bread]. Everybody cuts the bad out.* (p. 176, original emphasis)

Amanda's quote highlights that it is a human characteristic to remove the intolerable. For these young women, cutting serves to remove their pain and gives them some control.

Among the 20 young women who had self-injured, a common theme was that they felt a tension between wanting to feel alive and wanting to cut out the pain. This duality was integral to these young women's explanations for their self-injury.

The third explanation for the link between cutting and sexual abuse is that women can use self-injury as a way to regain some control over their bodies. I will refer to this explanation as *re-asserting control*. Like dissociation, control is a theme which abounds in the literature on self-injury (Adler and Adler 2011; Favazza 1998; Tyler et al. 2003). Strong (1998, p. xviii) asserts that cutting may "allow the tortured individual to play out the roles of victim, perpetrator, and finally, loving caretaker soothing self-inflicted wounds and watching them heal". This explanation is supported by the work of Suyemoto (1998) and Chandler (2012b), who found that for some self-injurers, having control of their body's injury, as well as being able to care tenderly for their wounds, was the purpose of this behaviour.

While injuring oneself as a way of controlling emotional turmoil seems paradoxical and counter to one's well-being, it needs to be understood in conjunction with the fact that these young women are also seeking control of their physical bodies, which have been ravaged by others. Suyemoto points out that "[s]elf-mutilation serves to define the boundaries of the self, as the skin is the most basic boundary between self and other" (1998, p. 546).

Wanting to remove emotional pain, as well as define and enforce the parameters of her own body, makes self-injury multifunctional. While none of the young women in this study spoke explicitly of self-injury as a form of self-care, Strong's explanations concerning the control of the body and control of emotions were themes that recurred throughout the interviews.

Sixteen-year-old Jessica explained, "I liked feeling like I could control things—I liked hurting myself." Similarly, Christina found relief in self-injury as a means to seek justice for her own perceived (and misguided) wrongdoings:

> It just made me feel better. I felt like I was punishing myself—I felt like it was my fault that he was doing it … I don't know, it got out pain, if you will.

It seemed that having control over the pain inflicted upon their bodies was part of the function of self-injury. Given the common experience of childhood abuse where their bodies were assaulted and their control stripped away, it is easy to understand why having this control of the body's boundaries is so desirable. While violating the body further as a way of releasing pain and garnering control seems nonsensical, it is pertinent to remember that many of these women loathed their bodies for "attracting" the sexual abuse.

For these young women, the need to be punished was a part of their everyday experience. Jazmine explained that while her cutting wasn't pleasurable, it was functional: "Sometimes I felt like I deserved it." Self-injury was not a sign of pathology; it was a method of coping.

The high prevalence of self-injury among this sample was an "accidental" discovery. I have explained that the behaviour these young women engaged in was not pathological. When asked why she self-injured, Ebony replied, "I'd just cut myself to kill the pain." When one understands the context in which she made this decision, and her need both to "feel alive" and to remove emotional pain, then her behaviour seems quite logical. These young women had engaged in self-injury to disrupt dissociation, to cut out emotional pain and to re-assert control over their own bodies. They had no psychopathology; they were experiencing the long-term effects of trauma.

From Self-Injury to Self-Medication

By the time of the interview, the young women were no longer engaged in self-injury. All of them had "graduated" from cutting to substance abuse. Katte was in a residential withdrawal unit for her substance use when I met her. When reflecting on the period of her life where self-injury was a common strategy, she explained:

At the time, [cutting] was the only thing that made me feel alive … it's true. It's kind of like, if you don't have drugs, what the fuck else are you going to do? You feel that shit about life. … Yeah. Like, I crave it [cutting] all the time. I wouldn't do it now, but I crave it because it was so good at the time—it's unreal.

Typically, people couldn't recall the specifics of either their entry into or exit from self-injury; rather, self-injury was something that they had moved into, and subsequently out of, without distinct delineation. Only two of the young women had made a conscious decision to stop cutting. Roxanne made a pragmatic explanation for her discontinuation and dryly explained that she "didn't need scars up my arms to remind me how shit my life is". Kate stopped because it was becoming an issue within her relationship:

My partner—who I am with now—his younger brother killed himself and it and, well, it wasn't that he was angry with me when I would do it, but it, well, it became too much of a problem. It was easier to not do it; to find another way to cope, because it was too much.

For Kate, this other way to cope was something which she could do with her partner: use drugs. The graduation from self-injury to substance use was typical, although it was less intentional for others than it was for Kate and Roxanne. When asking young women about their reasons for using drugs, there was a familiar sentiment being expressed. Roxanne explained her transition into problematic substance use:

I think the reason that I started using heroin was because I was either going to kill myself, or I was going to find something that was going to make me not kill myself, and at that point in time, as bad as it was, it helped. Well, it didn't help; but it helped.

Roxanne's insight shows that there was a distinct similarity in the functions of both self-injury and substance abuse, though the former always preceded the latter.

Mary was the only participant who still has episodes of self-injury, although these were less frequent:

I guess when I am really angry in myself, it's a way to vent that anger at yourself, the frustration, the self-pity. It's something I fall back on because it's one of the first things I did to cope with feeling really isolated and depressed and stuff … I did that before I tried drugs or anything. It's pretty easy to get addicted to, because—I know it's a cliché that everyone says about it—but it's the only thing that makes you feel some other way than what you are feeling.

Mary's explanation indicates the similarities in the function of self-injury and substance abuse. She shows that self-injury was her coping mechanism before drugs. This was a frequent narrative, and young women always moved from self-injury to substance abuse, never vice versa.

Jazmine also spoke about the gradual shift from self-injury to substance abuse and the purpose drugs served:

Well, if I am on drugs, I wouldn't cut—if that makes sense? 'Cause that's why I did them—so I wouldn't get sad. Well, you can get sad, but if I am on ecstasy or speed, obviously I am not really in reality at all; I am in another place, not really thinking about that stuff... I wasn't managing at all. Not just not managing school, I wasn't managing. That's why I was doing drugs—it was an escape.

KD: The drugs were the managing?

Yeah, they were the managing, because it was like, "I don't want to think about anything right now, so if I take some drugs, I won't have to".

For Jazmine, both cutting and substance abuse had helped her escape from her sadness. Jazmine's need to escape reality in order to survive was similar to Roxanne who had used drugs to stop herself from taking her own life. When these women were without support, their coping methods were self-injury and substance use:

To be honest, I can't imagine myself—the state I was in—dealing with what I was dealing with in any other way. I think that if I didn't do drugs I would be dead, to be honest. I would have committed suicide by now. There would have been another time in hospital, and I wouldn't have come out. Or I wouldn't have gone to hospital, if that makes sense?

Needing to escape reality and dull intolerable emotions were the reason these young women cut themselves, and they were also the reason they used drugs so aggressively. The similarities between young women's descriptions of the function of their self-injury and their substance use speak to a broader issue: their worlds were unbearably painful and they were attempting to dull the pain. Not only was self-injury logical when its function was understood, so too was the move from cutting to drug use.

In the interviews, it was clear that the young women felt stigmatised about their self-injury. Many were surprised to be asked what they liked about it—it was clear that they had not met many, if any, people who were accepting of the behaviour. The same level of stigma was not attached to their drug use. Among the broader youth population, it has already been established that recreational drug use is a normal activity (Duff 2005). For these young women, self-injury was a private activity that was done alone, whereas drug use was something that was done with partners, friends and family. These young women moved in a world where drug use was an accepted form of behaviour. Therefore, as they got older, it made sense to use drugs, rather than cutting, as a way of coping.

The young women were not seeking the recreational highs of ecstasy to enhance a night out in a club; they were seeking to stop the pain. Thus, they gravitated towards substances that had this pharmacological effect. Lisa's experience illustrates well the appeal of drugs that block the pain:

> *The problem is that I can still remember it [the sexual abuse]*
>   *KD: How have you managed since, to block it out?*
>   *Yeah, drinking or something. I don't know. It still doesn't make you feel much better. It does for a while, but it's still there.*

For Lisa, alcohol was soon replaced by heroin. When discussing the appeal of heroin, I observed that heroin is a "very numbing sort of drug—it's like a pain killer", to which she replied:

> *Yeah, I think that's the main thing that set it off in my brain. I didn't tell Mum for so long that I think I just needed some other way for trying to cope with it.*

Lisa's case highlights why the anaesthetic properties of depressant-type drugs held much appeal.

Ebony, after transitioning from self-injury, soon learnt that drugs could block out the pain of sexual abuse. The cost of drugs also saw her enact another lesson she'd subconsciously learnt in childhood: that her body was a commodity. When she was first kicked out, she ended up in the red light district of Kings Cross. During this time, drugs quickly became a major issue in her life as she struggled to cope. Ebony was despondent at her mother:

> *Mum knew too, and she didn't do anything. She always called me a bad kid but she doesn't [get it]. I tried to tell her why I've done what I've done, is because of, you know, that man. Everything I have done is because of that man ... I started everything when I was about 13. My first drug, heavy drug—I'm talking about heroin and stuff like that—was when I was homeless. One of the girls shot it up my arm for me ... I was 13 and she did it and I just thought, "This is so good", you know, just forgets everything and then, shortly after, I ended up having an $800 a day habit.*

Despite the problems which came from such a habit, the benefits of the drug use outweighed the negatives of raising the means to finance the habit. When asked what she liked about heroin, Ebony replied:

> *Everything. Just the tingle in the nose; you don't worry about anything; just everything—just being on the nod, yeah, I loved it, I loved drugs.*

She liked drugs that made her forget.

Her childhood had been filled with physical, sexual and emotional abuses by her stepfather, and she had been abandoned by her mother, leaving her without an adult in her life who could provide her with a safe place in the world. Ungar (2013) has established that relationships with strong positive adults are integral to a young person's resilience.

Similarly for Lisa, drugs were a way of managing life on the streets after years of sexual abuse in after-school care. Like self-injury, substance abuse was never an intended path for these young women but it was, in many ways, a highly effective way of coping.

By the time I met these women, all were seeking to move on from substance abuse. Lisa articulates this well when she explains that drug use was "just a fun thing to go and do when it wasn't serious, and then it turned serious and it wasn't fun anymore."

Conclusion

This chapter set out to "look below the surface" and to ask whether there was any link between self-injury and substance abuse. I began by reviewing two approaches that explain cutting. The first account views self-injury as evidence of pathological behaviour, whereas the second approach views self-injury as a strategy for coping with intense emotional pain. All 20 young women who had self-injured had experienced intense emotional pain, including 16 (80 per cent) who had been sexually abused as children and 14 (70 per cent) who felt abandoned by their mothers.

Focus then turned to the phenomenon of dissociation. This is a psychological defence mechanism that helps people to cope with abuse by separating mind from body. Emotional pain is internalised and the victim feels disconnected from her body or "without feeling". Slicing one's flesh with a blade made these women feel "alive". At the same time, it symbolised "cutting out the pain" and re-asserting control over their bodies.

As they got older, all of the young women moved on from cutting to substance abuse. In the interviews, it was clear that they felt stigmatised because they cut themselves, whereas there was less stigma associated with drug use. They started to mix in circles where drug use was an accepted recreational activity and drugs were easy to obtain. These young women had cut themselves to control emotional pain, and they used drugs for much the same purpose. Not only was self-injury logical when its function was understood, so too was the move from cutting to drug use as the women got older. For the women in this study, self-injury and substance abuse served the same purpose. They were ways of "cutting out the pain".

References

Adler, P. A., & Adler, P. (2011). *The tender cut: Inside the hidden world of self-injury*. New York: New York University Press.

Alexander, N., & Clare, L. (2004). You still feel different: The experience and meaning of women's self-injury in the context of lesbian or bisexual identity. *Journal of Community and Applied Social Psychology, 14*, 70–84.

American Psychiatric Association. (2013). *Diagnostic and statistical manual of mental disorders* (5th ed.). Arlington: American Psychiatric Association Publishing.

Cameron, J., Pennay, A., Reichert, T., Simpson, A., Wise, R., & Hall, K. (2012). *Making waves: An introduction to managing deliberate self-harm: A guide for AOD clinicians*. Victoria, Australia: Turning Point Alcohol and Drug Centre.

Chandler, A. (2012a). Inviting pain? Pain, dualism and embodiment in narratives of self-injury. *Sociology of Health and Illness., 35*(5), 716–730.

Chandler, A. (2012b). Self-injury as embodied emotion work: Managing rationality, emotions and bodies. *Sociology, 46*(3), 442–457.

Chandler, A., Myers, F., & Platt, S. (2011). The construction of self-injury in the clinical literature: A sociological exploration. *Suicide and Life Threatening Behaviours, 41*(1), 98–109.

Claes, L., & Vandereycken, W. (2007). Self-injurious behaviour: Differential diagnosis and functional differentiation. *Comprehensive Psychiatry, 48*, 137–144.

Crouch, W., & Wright, J. (2004). Deliberate self-harm at an adolescent unit: A qualitative investigation. *Clinical Child Psychology and Psychiatry, 9*(2), 185–204.

Duff, C. (2005). Party drugs and party people: Examining the "normalization" of recreational drug use in Melbourne, Australia. *International Journal of Drug Policy, 16*, 161–170.

Favazza, A. R. (1996). *Bodies under siege: Self- mutilation and body modification in culture and psychiatry.* Baltimore, MD: Johns Hopkins University Press.

Favazza, A. R. (1998). The coming of age of self-mutilation. *The Journal of Nervous and Mental Disease, 186*(5), 259–268.

Harris, J. (2000). Self-harm: Cutting the bad out of me. *Qualitative Health Research, 10*(2), 164–173.

Hodgson, S. (2004). Cutting through the silence: A sociological construction of self-injury. *Sociological Inquiry, 74*(2), 167–179.

Horne, O., & Csipke, E. (2009). From feeling too little and too much, to feeling more and less? A nonparadoxical theory of the functions of self-harm. *Qualitative Health Research, 19*(5), 655–667.

Klonsky, E. D., & Moyer, A. (2008). Childhood sexual abuse and non-suicidal self-injury. *The British Journal of Psychiatry, 192*(3), 166–170.

Levenkron, S. (1998). *Cutting: Understanding and overcoming self-mutilation.* New York: W. W. Norton.

Martin, G., Swannell, S. V., Hazell, P. L., Harrison, J. E., & Taylor, A. W. (2010). Self-injury in Australia: A community survey. *Medical Journal of Australia, 195*(9), 506–510.

National Institute of Mental Health. (n.d.). *Borderline personality disorder.* Rockville, MD: US Department of Health and Human Services.

Noddings, N. (2003). *Caring: A feminine approach to ethics and moral education* (2nd ed., Kindle ed.). Los Angeles: University of California Press.

Presson, B., & Rambo, C. (2016). Claiming resisting and exempting pathology in the identities of self-injurers. *Deviant Behavior, 37*(2), 219–236.

Strong, M. (1998). *A bright red scream.* London: Virago.

Suyemoto, K. L. (1998). The functions of self-mutilation. *Clinical Psychology Review, 18*(5), 531–554.

Tyler, K. A., Whitbeck, L. B., Hoyt, D. R., & Johnson, K. D. (2003). Self-mutilation and homeless youth: The role of family abuse, street experiences, and mental disorders. *Journal of Research on Adolescence, 13*(4), 457–474.

Ungar, M. (2013). The impact of youth-adult relationships on resilience. *International Journal of Child, Youth and Family Studies, 3*, 328–336.

6

Becoming a Man: Working-Class Masculinity, Machismo and Substance Abuse

Having explained more detail about the young women, the question remains: what about the boys? In this chapter I examine the intersection between masculinity and substance abuse in the lives of the young men in this study. To begin, the chapter reviews four concepts that will guide the empirical analysis. The concepts are working-class hegemonic masculinity, working-class machismo, and Erving Goffman's (1959) concepts of "front-stage" and "backstage" selves.

Following this, I examine a range of factors that helped shape the masculinity of the young men. The most important factors were the role of fathers in their lives, the examples provided by "dominant" males in their peer groups, their experiences in the homeless subculture and the criminal justice system.

After that, we go "backstage" and examine the connection between masculinity, emotional trauma and substance abuse. The chapter concludes that for these men, outbursts of uncontrolled anger and drug and alcohol abuse were different ways of dealing with emotional pain.

© The Author(s) 2016
K. Daley, *Youth and Substance Abuse*,
DOI 10.1007/978-3-319-33675-6_6

Four Concepts

Connell's (2005) concept of hegemonic masculinity has become the dominant paradigm in the theoretical literature on gender studies. Hegemonic masculinity is a concept that is used to identify and describe social practices that ensure the privileging of men and subordination of women and to explain the reproduction of these practices. The defining characteristics of hegemonic masculinity are male power, dominance, control and heterosexuality.

However, Connell points out that not all men exert a singular masculinity and that some masculinities hold more hegemonic power than others. Connell has emphasised that hegemonic masculinity does not infer that there is a singular dominant masculinity; rather, it may take a range of forms, particularly in societies where there are important class, ethnic or other social divisions. Thus, what constitutes "hegemonic masculinity" is context-dependent. As Connell explains:

> "Hegemonic masculinity" is not a fixed character type, always and everywhere the same. It is, rather, the masculinity that occupies the hegemonic position in a given pattern of gender relations, a position always contestable. (2005, p. 76)

In this chapter, I will use the concept of *working-class hegemonic masculinity* to refer to the cluster of characteristics that are typical of "mainstream" working-class masculinity. These ideas cohere around the following themes:

- a "proper" man has a job; he is a hard worker, a good provider and the main breadwinner in a family unit;
- a "proper" man believes in marriage, heterosexuality and "having a family";
- and a "proper" man should not show weakness or display emotion in the face of adversity.

Connell (2005) and Coles (2009) point out that these characteristics are not fixed because the construction of masculinity is an ongoing project for all men, and masculinity is both contested and reproduced. Nonetheless, the dominant understanding of mainstream working-class masculinity revolves around the idea that men are workers, breadwinners, heterosexual and do not display weakness or emotional pain. In this chapter, I will use the terms *working-class hegemonic masculinity* and *mainstream working-class masculinity* interchangeably.

The second concept that I will use is *working-class machismo*. Machismo refers to a public display of masculinity that emphasises toughness, bravado and an exaggerated show of assertive manliness. This is also referred to as "hyper-masculinity". Working-class culture that is characterised by machismo does *not* celebrate proper men as "hard workers", or "good providers". On the contrary, working-class machismo celebrates men as "outsiders", often engaged in dubious ways of earning money and taking part in activities that may be outside the law. These young men are in a working-class culture that is characterised by machismo and also celebrates heavy drug and alcohol use, where to be a big drinker or a heavy drug user (or both) is to be a "real" man.

A number of studies have pointed out that men from minority groups often construct a version of hegemonic masculinity that celebrates male strength and toughness as a distinctive characteristic of their minority group. For example, Trimbur (2011) undertook an ethnographic study of an urban boxing gym. His research explored the relationships between trainers and their young male boxers. Masculinity was a central theme. Trainers had a very clear understanding of how a "real man" ought to act: a proper man was a breadwinner who must be strong and resolute in the face of adversity. Trainers used an approach which they referred to as "tough love". Again, the absence of vulnerability characterised what it meant to "be a man" in the urban boxing gym.

Bourgois's (2002) ethnography of the street-based crack trade in East Harlem from the mid-1980s to early 1990s also drew attention to the role of physical toughness in the construction of hegemonic masculinity. Poor black males sought visible and confrontational expressions of power in the street scene, while simultaneously having virtually no power in the society which existed beyond their housing tenements. Bourgois wanted to understand how the young men subconsciously reconciled their broader powerlessness with their want for dignity and power (and thus masculinity) in what he describes as "inner-city street culture". He argues that there is "a complex and conflictual web of beliefs, symbols, modes of interaction, values, and ideologies that have emerged in opposition to exclusion from mainstream society. Street culture offers an alternative forum for autonomous personal dignity" (Bourgois 2002, p. 8).

There have also been studies of other marginalised working-class men that draw attention to the importance of "toughness" in working-class male culture. The importance of men being tough and not showing weakness is a central theme in Jewkes's (2005) ethnographic study of prisoners in the UK, and she pays particular attention to how men go to great lengths to present themselves as physically strong and resolute to other inmates and prison officers. De Viggiani (2012) also explored what he termed "masculine performances" in prison settings and discovered findings similar to Jewkes's.

The final two concepts that I will use to shape the empirical analysis are *front-stage* and *backstage* selves which draw from the writing of Erving Goffman (1959). Goffman's dramaturgical model proposes that how we behave and present ourselves in social interactions is governed by context-dependent cues such as social norms and cultural values. Goffman proposed that an individual's intention in a social "act" is to receive acceptance from their audience. This process is commonly referred to as "impression management". Continuing in the theatrical metaphor, Goffman described two dominant presentations of self: *front stage* and *backstage*. The former refers to the individual actor's "performance" of self in social situations ("on stage"), and the backstage self is one's real self when not on stage.

Several researchers who have explored masculinity and social class draw on Goffman's model of impression management. Jewkes (2005) undertook an ethnographic study with prisoners in the UK in which many of the men discussed the need to "act tough". Jewkes suggests that men in prison have two active masculinities which fit within Goffman's concepts of front stage and backstage. The front-stage masculinity among these prisoners was assertive and tough, and consciously performed. Simon, one of Jewkes's participants, explained, "You definitely have to wear a mask in prison—if you don't you're going to get eaten away ... You have to act tough. There's always the threat of violence" (2005, p. 46). However, when prisoners are presented with the opportunity to talk to a non-judgemental and impartial outsider, in this case a researcher, they let their front-stage mask drop and reveal their real selves.

De Viggiani (2012) also explored masculinity within prison settings and, like Jewkes, found Goffman's framework useful. He pays particular attention to how prisoners behave when they are front stage. De Viggiani found that prisoners must employ their "masculine'" persona when they are front stage so as to not reveal their vulnerability. The enactment of their front-stage masculinity is an attempt to present an aggressive, powerful masculinity that demonstrates male dominance and control.

Backstage masculinity is where the prisoner is "himself", a persona only revealed to trusted outsiders or when he is alone in his cell. This side of his personality reveals his emotions and vulnerabilities, which must be masked at all times when he is front stage and interacting with other prisoners. As Paul, a participant in Jewkes's study, explained, "The greatest tool a prisoner can have is to stay … in control and not show any vulnerability" (p. 59).

This chapter will use these four concepts—working-class hegemonic masculinity, working-class machismo, and Goffman's concepts of front stage and backstage—to shape the empirical analysis that follows.

First, we look front stage and examine how these young men grew up in a world where working-class hegemonic masculinity was taken for granted. Then we glimpse backstage, where another side of the men is revealed. Returning front stage, we see why the men adopted a new form of masculinity as they grew older. Finally, we step backstage again: all is not what it seems and the jigsaw "falls into place".

Front Stage: Working-Class Hegemonic Masculinity

The first role models that most young men have of what it is like to be a "man" are provided by their parents. In this section I examine some of the core messages about masculinity that these young men learnt from parents. These "messages" varied in a range of ways, but one constant was that an adult male is a worker and a provider, despite that many of the young men who held these views had been raised by single mothers. Another constant was that men should be "tough" or "strong" and not engage in excessive displays of emotion.

Mothers and Sons

Nearly all of the young men were raised with, and often exclusively by, their mothers. Only seven (20 per cent) of the young men were brought up in conventional nuclear families where their parents remained together until they finished school. The other 28 (80 per cent) came from families where their parents had either divorced or separated or their mother was a single parent and their biological father had never been present.

The young men seemed to take to take it for granted that their relationship with their mother was a constant in their lives, even where there was sometimes conflict between them. There was a tacit understanding that: "Mum would always be there".

Despite many absent fathers, the young men's discussions about parents often focused primarily on them, particularly the issue of their parents' marriage breakdown. Some had watched their own father beating up their mother and this was very confronting for the young men: they were too small to protect their mothers from harm; at the same time they were learning that adult men beat up wives and girlfriends.

Some of the mothers had mental health issues or substance abuse problems and these created difficulties at home. However, the young men were often sympathetic towards their mothers. Shawn, who had moved in and out of care, and whose baby brother died after his mother forgot to feed him (which led to her imprisonment), showed much compassion towards his mother, despite her failings as a parent:

> *A lot of people don't understand why I don't hate my mum for some of the things that she has done—but it was the only way she knew how to do it.*

Shawn was aware that he and his mother had experienced intergenerational poverty—his mother had also been raised in state care—and the structural disadvantage that this caused.

Jai's story was similar. His mother was never violent, but she neglected her children when she was substance affected. When Jai was in primary school, his mother died of an overdose of heroin and benzodiazepines. He explained that her drug use was heaviest when her boyfriend was violent:

> *That's why she started doing drugs, to numb the pain; to numb the memories ... I understand why she did drugs; but when she was off of them she loved us all to bits and she'd do anything for us, so that's the things that I like to remember.*

Will and his mother fought a lot and she had placed a restraining order against him. Despite this, she did not report him to the police when he came to the house to visit his sister. Will had insight into his volatile relationship with his mother:

> *I've got problems, and she's got problems—and we've both got really big problems ... my mum still does care, in a way. Yeah, she still does, but she just doesn't show it. It feels like she doesn't [care], but she does.*

Will's goal for the future was to have a good relationship with his mother, although he realised that they would both have to change to make this possible.

Michael's parents separated when he was three and he lived with his mother full-time until he reached adolescence. He then oscillated between his mother's and his father's places. The typical pattern would be that he would push the boundaries at his mother's and reject her attempts at enforcing rules. Then she would insist that he live with his father who was much stricter. Nonetheless, Michael was closer to his mother than to his authoritarian father: "I wasn't scared of Mum. I used to laugh when she'd tell me off."

Simon also oscillated between his parents' homes, but he was more comfortable talking about personal things to his mum. From an early age, the men had learned the heteronormative ideal that women are more caring than men and that men should not display their emotions. This was apparent in all of the men in the sample, regardless of whether or not they were heterosexual.

Fathers and Sons

Some of the young men retained connections with their fathers even though they did not live with them. In some cases, they stayed with them occasionally when they were growing up or sometimes they lived with them intermittently during their teenage years. When fathers were involved in their sons' lives, they provided role models of adult male behaviour.

Michael's father had an expectation that his son ought to "become a man, get a job". Michael explained that men are expected "get up in the mornings … go to work every day". The understanding that a man should work hard and be a breadwinner was seen by most of the young men as a fundamental requirement to be a "proper man". This view was apparent even in cases where the young men had not ever seen that modelled. There was an intuitive knowledge, somehow absorbed through socio-cultural norms that their father was "failing" at his fundamental tasks. Although the men were able to forgive the father for not being emotionally supportive (that was seen as their mother's role), they felt their fathers were meant to have provided material means such as housing and income.

Even though most women are now employed in the labour force (ABS 2012), this binary of men as providers and women as carers is a fundamental characteristic of working-class hegemonic masculinity. The young men took it for granted that they would be workers and providers. When asked about their futures, the men's answers were remarkably similar. Andrew wanted "to have a house … a good job and a girlfriend". Michael was also sure and succinct: "I want to have a job … I want to get married. I want to have kids." Beau had similar goals: "To have a job, to get a nice house. Just the basics."Nearly all of the young men wanted to get married and they all expected to be the main breadwinner.

Damian's father had instilled similar beliefs in his son through the example set by his own behaviour. Damian father had always risen early and was renowned for working long hours. According to Damian, his father had a "go hard" attitude to all aspects of his life. He had been involved in competitive cycling and his sporting success was something Damian had sought to emulate.

There was an absence of affection between many of the fathers and their sons. Damian could not recall his father showing affection towards him. His father's sense of how he should be as an adult male was closely tied to his ideas about hard work and physical "toughness". Demonstrating affection to another male, including his own son, was simply not part of his father's emotional repertoire.

Luke's father had a white-collar occupation, but he also did not discuss his emotions with his son or display affection towards him. Luke's relationship with his father lacked warmth. His father was not intentionally cold or unloving; however, he spent long hours at work and appeared not to have learnt how to demonstrate affection to his wife or children. Luke's father was genuinely surprised when his marriage failed, because he felt he had fulfilled his obligations by being a good provider and faithful husband.

Shawn's parents had separated when he was an infant, and he had been brought up by his mother. He went to live with his father when he was 12 years old, soon after his mother was incarcerated. His father epitomised working-class hegemonic masculinity. He worked hard and he was a good provider. He was also emotionally disconnected from his children. After Shawn's baby brother, who had a different father, died from malnourishment and dehydration, Shawn's father explained to him that he had "one week to get over it" and then to never mention it again.

Shawn also had to hide his homosexuality from his father because, "[i] f Dad found out I'd end up dead in the ground". Shawn's father provided stable housing and food for his family; however, his way of being a man was defined by heterosexuality, breadwinning and the denial of emotions.

Much of the time young men learnt what it was to be a man almost by osmosis, because the role models of adult masculinity were all around. Sometimes fathers also told sons explicitly what was expected of them. Michael recalled his father telling him:

> *Just be a man. What are you being lazy for? Sitting in bed and smoking choof ... Who the fuck do you think you are? ... Get a job!*

The young men took it for granted that an adult man should be a "worker and a provider". How they might achieve this was not ever discussed.

A Glimpse Backstage

Family Breakdown: "That Burst My Fucking Bubble"

In this section we get the first glimpse of the backstage persona of these young men. Family breakdown had a lasting effect on them—much more so than the young women. "Real men" do not display their emotions, but there was an indicator that these young men were not handling their emotions well.

When I asked Jerry why he was getting into so much trouble, he reluctantly replied: "I really don't know. I was just a dick head. I don't know. Maybe it had something to do with my parents splitting up when I was young."

Luke was more affected by his parents' separation than his sisters were. He explained that at the time of the divorce, he did not want to attend counselling even though the rest of his family did. At the time he claimed that he was "fine":

My parents split up when I was really young; when I was about six or seven … I remember that my brother and sister were crying, but I just took it in. I didn't really show any emotions, I didn't do anything.

Later, it turned out that he was not fine at all. "It really killed me—it did—but I just didn't show anything at the time. I just bottled it up."

Jake believed that he came from a "normal" family, but this rapidly came undone when his parents announced they were splitting up:

It was a bit rough in grades five and six because my parents broke up at one point … I had always thought that I had this normal home life. My parents always seemed happy. And then when the tables turned in grade five and all this shit was coming to the surface, then it all started piecing together … that burst my fucking bubble, it was horrible. All I wanted was a normal home life and when I looked around, it really wasn't normal at all.

During his parents' divorce, Jake discovered that his father smoked cannabis and he began smoking it too.

Jakey's (distinct from Jake) parents had separated about a year before I interviewed him. He was dividing his time between them and the break-up was reasonably amicable. This is noteworthy because his father's infidelity was the impetus for the separation. When his parents first separated, his father moved in with his new partner and had little contact with Jakey:

> *I have never really been close with my dad, so not having him around isn't—well, I wish they were still together—but not having him around is not really a big thing.*

I was unconvinced: on the one hand his father's absence was "not a big thing", but on the other, he also wished they "were still together". Following his parents' separation, Jakey's drug use escalated, and it was his drug problem that saw his mother and father begin to communicate again. Jakey and his sister both hoped their parents would reunite. When he was front stage, Jakey claimed "indifference" about his parents' marriage breakdown, but backstage his views were quite different.

Jahl's case was different in two respects. First, he had never had a relationship with his biological father but had been very close to his stepfather. Second, he was not "fine" when his mother and stepfather separated. On the contrary, he was "devastated". Like Jake, Luke and Jakey, he handled the separation badly:

> *They broke up when I was about eight and then I was a bad kid straight away … When they broke up my life got bad from there.*

The dynamics of family breakdown are complex. What was common for these young men is that they had not yet worked through the emotions associated with their parents' separation. Many had declared that they were "fine" when they were not, and many of these young men were dealing with confused emotions and internal conflicts associated with their parents' separation. Young men were often faced with the dilemma that the person they had assumed to be a "good man" was perhaps not so good after all.

Michael's parents had separated because his father had had an extramarital affair. His father was a "womaniser", and in many ways this trait was something Michael admired. He spoke about his father's appreciation of women's company, and how he sought to treat women "properly". At the same time, what constituted "properly" was largely ambiguous:

> *He broke up with one fiancée, and got another fiancée. He broke up with her, and then he was seeing a few different girlfriends … he's out on the weekends with girls … what a sick cunt!*

Despite his admiration for his father's liaisons with women and his own appreciation of women, when I suggested that he takes after his father, Michael emphasised that he "wasn't that bad" and explained emphatically:

> *There's a difference between me and my dad: my dad would cheat, I would never cheat. I honestly wouldn't … You only need one girl.*

The pain of his father's infidelity had left a permanent impression on him. Yet in other parts of the interview, Michael was at pains to emphasise that his father was a "good bloke". It remained unclear whom Michael was trying to convince of this. Michael was faced with the dilemma that perhaps his father was not such a "good bloke" after all.

There were also young men who had grown up without fathers. In some cases, they were indifferent about the men who were their biological fathers. In other cases, they had tried to make contact with them, typically with high hopes for what this would bring.

Brandon had not had contact with his father for many years. Nonetheless, after becoming homeless, Brandon wanted to rebuild his relationship with his father, optimistic about their future relationship. When they met, it turned out that his father was a very heavy drinker and he kept calling Brandon by another son's name. Brandon's anger quickly escalated to the point of physical violence. On one occasion, the police were called to separate the two men. Brandon told me his final words to his father:

> *I just told him the truth. I said, "I'll tell you the truth … you're an arsehole, that's what you are. You drink too much. My brothers said you've changed but to me you just seem much worse."*

It is also important to recognise that young men make judgements about how well other men behave. This was obvious in Michael's judgement that his father was both a "good bloke" and a "sick cunt" and in Brandon's judgement that his father was an "arsehole". In the same way that people make situated choices, they also make situated judgements about how well other men "perform" masculinity.

So far, we have seen that these young men took it for granted that a proper man is a hard worker, a good provider and the main breadwinner in a family unit. Along with marriage and heterosexuality, these are central tenets of working-class hegemonic masculinity. Closely tied to this was their understanding men should not show their emotions. However, we have also glimpsed backstage and are able to see that things may not be as "OK" as the young men might say on first asking.

Front Stage: Friends, Drugs and Machismo

Now we return front stage. First we examine their friendships and drug use in high school, and then we turn to their encounter with machismo.

The "Wrong Crowd"

The young women rarely spoke of friends, and when they did, it was often in the past tense—friendships which had ended as drug use escalated. The opposite was true for the young men: sometimes the need to build friendships was the primary motivation to begin using drugs.

In their four studies of youth in Britain's working-class area of Teesside, MacDonald et al. (2011) found that youth who shared a combined "career" of drug using and crime were disconnected from more "mainstream" peers and, in turn, entered a social network where drug use and crime were entrenched. This phenomenon was apparent here also.

After migrating from Vietnam, Pailin went to an Australian high school. Unfortunately, he had little grasp of English. Classrooms were impossible for him to "fit in", but he soon noticed the group of boys who were skipping classes. This group was appealing to Pailin, who wanted to escape from the classroom and also wanted friends:

> *I couldn't speak properly, and I met the wrong group of friends. I wanted to fit in, I guess. I knew no one, so I guess I just wanted to fit in.*

These were the "wrong crowd" and we will meet them many times in the narratives of the young men.

James had undiagnosed dyslexia which hampered his learning:

> *I got bullied around school because of my dyslexia and learning disabilities and that's why I ended up hanging out with the wrong crowd.*

Shawn had changed schools many times and he was placed into a remedial class:

> *and that's how I got into the wrong crowd. ... all of the kids who were stuffing up and not doing the right thing were all put into the one class and kept separate from everyone else. We had a different lunch area from everyone else—we were kept completely separate.*

The "wrong crowd" were not doing well academically and they were into drug use, some petty crime and occasional violence. Andy, like Shawn, had changed schools many times and he too had met the "wrong crowd":

> *I went to four different high schools from year seven to year eight. I went to one in Berwick, one in Narre, got kicked out of the one in Narre and the one in Berwick, then I went to one in Doveton, and then I moved out of the area so I went to Pakenham. School wasn't that good, getting into fights ... bullying ... I started hanging around the wrong crowd, the smokers down the back of the oval, mixing with the wrong crowd, hanging out with a few of them, getting into crimes after school, smoking a bit of weed after school, getting kicked out of school for smoking weed, those sort of things.*

The wrong crowd usually smoked marijuana. As we saw earlier, Pailin sought out "the smokers" because they did not attend classes. However, to join the "wrong crowd", Pailin needed to engage in their recreational practices:

I needed to become one of the cool kids who smoked at school and that's what I turned into.

For some it took time to adjust to this new activity. Jake referred to his introduction to drugs as his "apprenticeship". He didn't know what hash was when he was given cookies containing it:

I was like, "What the fuck are these pins and needles through my body?". I didn't like it ... I didn't try choof again until I had a bong. I didn't like it but I kept forcing myself to smoke to be cool. Literally, smoking to be cool.

Jake's explanation of not enjoying his early experiences of drug use was typical of a minority of the young men, but they continued to smoke because they wanted to be part of the group.

Similarly, Jakey did not enjoy drugs on his first introduction. At school, he made some friends who were "stoners":

I used to do bongs with them, but I hated it. I couldn't stand it. I used to just do it, not peer pressure ... but it was kind of like, "Oh yeah, I'll do it", but I always hated it.

He stopped hanging out with those friends because he did not want to smoke. Nevertheless, Jakey's initial need to make friends was still there. He later met another friend and found himself smoking cannabis with him.

As most of the young men explained, the "wrong crowd" was a welcoming group. Pailin's inability to speak fluent English was barely noticed so long as he participated in the group's social practices. Some men liked the "wrong crowd" because there they met other young people who often had disadvantaged backgrounds like themselves. Chris shed light on this:

Wherever somebody feels they fit in, or feel comfortable with that group of people, then they want to do what those people are doing. That's pretty much what it is ... It's good to fit in somewhere, it's good to be a "type" of person rather than different to everybody … There's nothing better than meeting someone who is like you on almost every level … Smoking choof was about fitting in and I don't regret it at all 'cause I have ended up having some great friends.

The young men liked the wrong crowd because it was here that they met people who were like them "on almost every level". Their childhoods had contributed to them feeling like "outcasts" and they gravitated towards friends who were "outsiders" like themselves.

Others joined the wrong crowd because they wanted to be "part of the action". Michael explained the attraction succinctly:

You just want to be a part of it—they are the macho boys … they were punching-on … they were the cool kids so I wanted to fit. Everything they would do I wanted to do.

Josh said matter-of-factly: "I just wanted to get in with a group of people that punched on with other people."

Unemployment, Homelessness and Crime

Earlier, we saw that mainstream working-class masculinity emphasises the importance of having a job and being a good provider. However, two-thirds (66 per cent) of the men had left school before Year 10, and another 20 per cent left school at the end of Year 10. Most of these young men became unemployed.

By the time these young men left school, they were all involved with the "wrong crowd", but the social composition of the "wrong crowd" was changing. Now they were mainly unemployed youth, engaged in regular drug use, often taking part in criminal activity, and many of them were homeless.

The young men were also moving into a subculture where there was much more emphasis on the machismo characteristics of working-class masculinity. Machismo refers to a public display of masculinity. Typically, it emphasises toughness, bravado, aggression and an exaggerated show of assertive manliness (Jewkes 2005). It downplays the importance of paid work and celebrates other male characteristics. The values encapsulated in machismo appealed to these unemployed teenagers.

Mick told how he started to meet people in the "wrong crowd" who were into criminal activity:

Then I met a lot of criminals that went there, a lot of fighters that went there and stuff. I shared my experiences with them and then they were like "Oh, so you're a little sick cunt are ya? Come on join us!"

He began to hang out with them and got into "a fair few blues. Yeah, it got real hectic".

Michael recalled an incident which perhaps epitomises the violence that is characteristic of working-class machismo:

Like I remember a fight ... Like, 30 of us jumped off a train. Fifteen ran from that direction, and about 10 popped out from cars, and there was 15 of them, and they were punching on and we literally smashed them all. I think me and my mate were the only ones to drop. One person, one of my mates was hit with a pole like five times, and he was harder, and he just smashed him, and everyone was just swinging at like five different people, and they were just cool kids.

He was proud to have been involved: "Everything they did I wanted to do."

Jerry remembered his time in the graffiti gangs: "I just looked up to all these older guys who are all pretty much in jail now." The "wrong crowd" was an amorphous group who appeared to turn up both everywhere and nowhere. Wherever the wrong crowd was, drugs, violence and crime were always "in the mix".

Almost 70 per cent (24 of 35) of the young men had been involved with the criminal justice system, 10 of whom had been incarcerated. The number who had been in prison was particularly high given that in Victoria, custodial sentences are generally a last resort and they usually follow non-custodial interventions such as Youth Supervision Orders and Drug Diversion Orders which seek to place the young persons under the supervision of Youth Justice services without imprisoning them. The aim is to have reduced recidivism and higher rates of rehabilitation. The typical route that led these young men to have contact with the justice system was a series of charges, most commonly for assault or theft.

Mick grew up with a firm understanding that violence between men was sometimes necessary, even between fathers and sons, but violence against women was never acceptable. His father had instilled this into him:

> *My dad said, "If you ever hit a woman, I'll break your arms, break your legs and I'll break your neck." I've just learnt, never touch a woman.*

When I met Mick, he was in a withdrawal unit. He explained to me that he had a history of quite extreme violence and aggression: an "uncontrollable rage". However, he explained that this rage, although exacerbated during withdrawal, never extended to breaching his father's instruction, suggesting that his rage was indeed controllable. Violence against women was abominable, but violence against other men was an essential part of "being a man".

Mick had a long history of violent encounters with other men, both inside and outside of school. As a consequence, he had a great deal of contact with the police and had accrued multiple charges for assaults and burglaries in his teenage years. He had spent two months in custody and was likely to be incarcerated in the future on other charges that were still outstanding. Despite his increasing criminal record, he did not question his entrenched view that violence was an inherent aspect of masculinity.

Andreas also spoke about violence and crime as an everyday aspect of manhood. His discussion about his impending incarceration was as casual as a conversation about the weather:

> *I just keep getting arrested for stuff… I've got court on Thursday, I have a fair chance of being locked up. So I don't know if rehab's gonna work. … I've got the choice, probably Fulham prison or Port Philip prison. So I will go to Port Philip, 'cause that's where my mates are.*

Many of his peer group were already incarcerated, and his brother also had a criminal record. The way he remarked—somewhat surprised—that he "kept getting arrested" reflected just how normalised violence was for him. Being arrested was something that happened to him—seemingly disconnected from his behaviour. Violence was, after all, "just the way men deal with things". For Andreas, his brother and his friends, involvement in the criminal justice system was part of a man's life. Violence and incarceration were rites of passage; they were the expected path for young men, for "tough" men, at least. And for these young men, a "tough" man was a "real" man.

Not all of the young men endorsed this extreme form of machismo. Jake was also held in a youth detention centre on remand and it was here that he saw himself as different from the other young people. He was witness to the excessive displays of hyper-masculinity that de Viggiani (2012) and Jewkes (2005) found to be typical in prisons, but Jake did not endorse this behaviour. His rejection of the jailhouse machismo set him apart from many of the other young men. Doing this was sufficiently unusual that even he felt the need to explain why he was different from other males: they were "hotheads, fuck-heads, egotistical maniacs", and he was not. Valkonen and Hänninen (2012) point out that while some men distance themselves from the dominant form of masculinity, it still remains a point of reference for them. We can see this here for Jake.

When I asked the young men about their entry into criminal activity, few could recall a distinct first event. For many of them, there had been a spate of charges, typically robbery, resisting arrest, theft, assault and possession of drugs, that had led to youth supervision orders, probation, bonds and custodial sentences. They seemed to have transitioned into violent and aggressive offenders as a by-product of being entrenched in a subculture where violence and crime were intrinsic to being a man. These young men knew they lived in a world where violence was illegal, but it was not understood as "wrong". Of course, these young men were making choices about how they acted out their masculinity—as we saw above, Mick would never hit a woman—but the young men were still constrained by their understanding of what it was to be a man.

Throughout the fieldwork, I took note of how normalised crime and violence were. The young men had no reticence over disclosing their histories—they did not feel it an unusual aspect of their biography. In contrast, the young women had been cautious when first disclosing self-injury. Most women tried to establish whether I viewed their behaviour as stigmatised, before revealing their story. There was no such reticence on the part of the young men talking about engaging in crime and violence. It was an accepted, and acceptable, part of their lives. The young men's accounts of their exploits drew on exaggerated stereotypes about masculinity. They did not perceive their exploits as remarkable because they lived in worlds where they were utterly unremarkable—to be violent was to be a man. However, as we will see in the next section, this is only part of the story.

Stepping Backstage: Young Men and Their Emotions

Trauma

Earlier, it was pointed out that Goffman's (1959) dramaturgical model proposes that when others are present, all people are "actors" who engage in "impression management". Continuing in the theatrical metaphor, Goffman described two dominant presentations of self: "front stage" and "backstage".

I will now use Goffman's theatrical metaphor to draw attention to how the men's front-stage presentations of themselves revolved around the idea that men should be "hard", "tough" and not display emotion. At the same time, many of them had a backstage understanding of themselves that was different: it revealed vulnerability.

Like many insights into human behaviour, this story begins with an unexpected event—an interview that at first appeared to provide few insights into my research question shed considerable light on the phenomenology of the young men's substance abuse.

Larry was a complex young man both younger and older than his 20 years implied. I met Larry when he was staying in a residential withdrawal unit. His behaviour and demeanour showed him to be an angry young man whose incessant pacing and fidgeting made it clear that he was also highly anxious. His tone was loud and mannerisms were dominating. I had met him a number of times when I had been "hanging around", and I was surprised when he stated that he would like to be interviewed.

Larry's interview was consistent with my assumptions about him: he swore a lot to punctuate his sentences and spoke mostly about fighting and asserting himself over other young men. He seemed to need to accentuate his toughness and aggression. I listened to endless stories about various standover tactics, his bravado and his violence. I continued to work through the interview schedule, taking notes, but concluded that I was learning nothing new.

Larry mentioned his mental health issues early on in the interview. He seemed to accept that drugs had a psychopharmacological effect on him that was considerably different from that of his peers. This had come to the fore when he was involuntarily admitted as a psychiatric inpatient with presentations of psychosis after consuming party drugs at a music festival. He had previously been seeing a youth mental health service but had never been admitted as an inpatient. Larry's stay in the hospital was a pivotal point in his life, although not because there was any profound improvement in his mental health. First, being away from his friends forced him to evaluate the foundations of these friendships where drug use was a key part of their social activity. While he felt better in this period of abstinence, he was simultaneously aware that if he was to continue with an abstemious lifestyle, this could come with the cost of losing his friends. Talking about this prospect evoked tears from him. Just as I had thought the interview was nearing an end, Larry's tears signalled the beginning of deeper revelations.

I am sure that he had not intended to cry in front of me—in front of anyone, I suspect—but once the floodgates opened, the torrent of tears washed away his tough, macho exterior revealing how he really felt. His "front-stage" persona was overcome by grief and his "backstage" self was revealed.

Apart from the fear of losing his friends, the second and most critical explanation to why Larry's time in the hospital was so profound was because he had met a girl there—Bec:

She was in there for depression. She, she cut herself, up-ways [which indicates suicide rather than self-injury]. I sussed it out. I didn't ask too many questions at the start. I thought it was just depression. I didn't click on that much. We just clicked. We hooked up. I got the story out of her, eventually. It was really hard for her to tell me, but I forced it out of her. She was raped when she was 16 ... she never got over it. Two years later, she started cutting herself ... Fuck, I tried to be calm [when she was telling me]. Not raging. Maybe I should have raged.

I don't know. I never really raged with her. But shit, she told me, man she told me, "You've got to find someone else. I love you, don't get me wrong, but I can't live, I can't live anymore". That's basically what she said to me, yeah [long pause] … she done it in the hospital. The third time she got readmitted.

Larry had been crying for a while now, but at this point he started sobbing. However, he kept on talking about this issue as the grief was, quite literally, pouring out of him:

She called me the night before she did it, like final goodbye sort of shit, but I didn't know what she was doing. That was the thing with her, she always had a smile on her face. Then I copped a call a week later, she's on life support. I didn't really get it, I thought she was fighting for her life [psychologically]. That's what her mum told me, "She's in Emergency, she's fighting for her life". And I'm like, "Yes, I know that", but I didn't really get the message … I didn't get it. Another week later and I hear, "Rebecca passed away". Just like that. I wasn't right after that.

By this point, Larry's sobbing was so uncontrollable that he was unable to speak. I asked him if he would like to stop the interview, but he was adamant that he wanted to continue. I told him that he was in a safe space and that I was comfortable with him crying. I sat quietly, allowing him to vent his grief. After a few minutes, he was ready to speak again. Without prompting, he began again:

The first time I heard the news, I was devastated. I didn't know what to do. I felt like a dog because I didn't really cry. I felt something, but I was like, "What's wrong with me? I can't even cry?" Like, I would get teary, but I couldn't even, I couldn't even bawl.

Larry had never grappled with the experience of death before, let alone suicide, and Rebecca was someone whom he cared about deeply. He had no idea how to handle grief or to deal with the intense emotions that welled up inside him.

He had tried to speak to his friends about Bec's suicide, but this was futile. They offered comments such as "Suicide is selfish" and "She was ugly anyway". Larry's friends did not mean to be contemptuous; rather, they were young men and also living in a world where emotional trauma should not affect a "real man". They too did not know what to say or do. Larry had no one to turn to, and his drug use, violence and mental health symptoms escalated. It was his interview which finally signalled the similarities between my male participants: the young men's ability to experience their emotions was deeply constrained by their notions of masculinity.

Death was a common part of these young men's life histories, with ten of the young men having lost a parent, best friend or partner. Jerry's best friend died in a motorcycle accident when he was 18. Inexperienced at grieving, Jerry began managing the heavy emotional toll through drug use. It was almost immediately after his best friend's death that Jerry's heroin use escalated. Talking about his feelings was impossible when he did not have a vocabulary to express them, but heroin killed the pain immediately:

> I couldn't really talk about it. I found it so hard to talk about. I've only just started talking about it in the last few months.

Jerry acknowledged that he had not coped with grief: "I was really close to him [best friend] ... and I was just fucked."

Andy had also lost his best friend and struggled with understanding it:

> My best mate passed away last year and he's the one who taught me respect, manners, and all that stuff. It was hard ... he got hit by a truck. He had a heart attack before he died ... I didn't cope with it. He was my best mate, that passed away ... I was with him for two years. I was always told you could never make a good mate in a refuge, and I met this guy at a refuge and we were best buddies, we went everywhere together. Christmas, birthdays, New Year, and then he ends up passing away.

Andy's narrative alludes to why his grief was felt so sharply—his best friend was his only key support. The death of a friend is not something teenagers typically experience. The intense emotions were overwhelming. While grief is an unwanted intrusion in anyone's life, most seek comfort from their loved ones, but Andy did not have anyone to care for him.

Shawn had been on a road trip with his mother when his infant brother died. When they got to a petrol station, Shawn checked on his brother in the back seat to find him dead. The baby weighed less at his death than at his birth and the case was subject to a coronial inquiry. When I interviewed Shawn, it had been six years since the event, and he was still deeply traumatised by the experience. Shawn had been given no time and no support to grieve properly. Following his brother's death, his mother was jailed and Shawn was placed into the care of the state. Later, he was reunited with his father, but we saw earlier that his father had given him one week to be sad and after that he was to not raise the topic again. A few months later, 12-year-old Shawn began using heroin.

Several young men had lost a parent. Clark, Jai and Jackson had also lost their mothers, and Will's father died when he was in Year 8. Two years later, Will's 17-year-old stepbrother also died. Asiah, a refugee who had fled war with his sister, did not know if his parents were alive. Not only had these young men lost people upon whom they depended, but this was compounded by the fact that none of these young men had the support needed to deal with the intense grief that accompanies the death of a loved one.

It's More Common Than You Think

Table 6.1 attempts to quantify the number of young men who had experienced various types of traumatic events. This is a fairly crude way of measuring the extent of trauma in young people's lives, because it does not take into account the intensity of the experience, the length of time that the traumatic event lasted or, indeed, whether the young person had multiple experiences of that particular type of trauma. Despite these limitations, Table 6.1 provides an indicator of the frequency of the trauma experienced by these men.

Table 6.1 shows that three-quarters (86 per cent) of the young men had experienced homelessness and 69 per cent had been involved in the criminal justice system. Many came from homes where their parents had serious problems: nearly half (46 per cent) had a parent with a mental illness, and nearly half (46 per cent) had a parent with a drug problem. Two-fifths (46 per cent) had been in contact with child protection,

Table 6.1 Number of males with various experiences of trauma

	N = 35	%
Experienced homelessness	30	86
Involvement in justice system	24	69
Parent with drug problem	16	46
Parent with mental illness	16	46
State care and protection	14	40
Death of friend or relative	10	29
Bullying at school	9	26
Abused as a child	9	26
Developmental disorder	8	21
Suicide attempt	6	17
Refugee	2	6
	140	

and others had experienced a range of other traumas in their childhood, including child abuse (26 per cent). One-fifth (21 per cent) had a developmental disorder that affected their learning—typically attention deficit hyperactivity disorder (ADHD) or dyslexia. Another one-quarter (26 per cent) had experienced bullying at school and five of the young men grew up caring for a mentally ill parent.[1] Damian explained that some days he would not go to school because he was worried that his mother might commit suicide.

Just under half (45 per cent) of the men had experienced either two or three of these trauma types, and almost the same number (42 per cent) had experienced four or more (Table 6.2). Three people had experienced none of them, but two had serious mental health issues and the other was traumatised by his parents' separation. The troubles of the young men were diverse, but in the next section I show how they managed emotional pain in similar ways.

Managing Emotional Pain

The sharp contrast between Larry's "tough" exterior and his later uncontrollable sobbing highlighted the fact that the hyper-masculinity expected of these young men normally prevented them from displaying

---

[1] The number of people who had witnessed family violence growing up was not known, thus not included in this table.

Table 6.2 Number of trauma types experienced by men	N = 35	%
None	3	9
One	1	3
Two or three	16	57
Four or more	15	31
	35	100

their emotions. We saw earlier that Larry felt "devastated" when he heard the Bec had committed suicide: "I didn't know what to do. I felt like a dog because I didn't really cry." In the previous chapter, I explained how young women who had been raped internalised intense emotional stress such that they felt "numb". Larry did the same when Bec committed suicide; he internalised his overwhelming emotional pain, experiencing dissociation. The interview had given him an opening to release that pain and it literally poured out of him in an uncontrolled torrent of weeping.

As the interview with Larry drew to a close, I asked him how he was feeling, to which he replied: "Yeah, better." He then spoke about how "pressure" had been relieved by expressing so much emotion. He felt better having allowed the pain "to flow out of him". The following week when I was back in the withdrawal unit, I made a point of checking in on Larry to see how he was doing. He greeted me warmly and thanked me again "for letting me download on you".

These young men inhabited a public world where their masculinity was defined by being "tough", aggressive and, sometimes, angry. The inability to talk about a much broader array of human emotion meant they often could not find words to express their feelings. For example, Brandon said:

> I feel lots of weird things, but I don't actually know what they are [i.e. anxiety], so it's hard when I go to talk to a counsellor or something because they ask me all these questions, "Have you got this?", "Have you got that?", "Do you feel this?", "Do you feel that?", and I don't know.

According to Jerry, after his best mate died he felt "numb": "I couldn't talk about it. I found it so hard to talk about it."

The young men often did not have the words to express the emotions that they were experiencing, and like the young women they had often internalised emotional pain. Not having the words to talk about their feelings allowed the pain to build up, and they released it through angry outbursts often involving violence.

Will could not explain why he ended up smashing things when he was depressed rather than talking about his problems. When his mother had tried to punish him by taking away his computer games, he had responded by kicking a hole in the wall. Similarly, during an argument, his stepfather ripped a poster of Will's wall. Will then pushed him down the stairs—this led to police intervention and involvement with the criminal justice system.

Brandon had experienced similar uncontrolled anger:

> *I get depressed all the time. I get upset over nothing. I get upset over what's happened, and then it goes to anger and I blackout and whatever happens, happens ... I've smashed a lot of things, a few people—I'm always having trouble with cops.*

Mick, who had a history of violent encounters with men, would deliberately pick a fight to release internal tension:

> *I'd go to a pub or whatever, pick on someone, wait until they'd fight me. I'd get smashed—I didn't care; I loved it. I loved being hurt so much 'cause it relieved all the tension out of me and all that.*

Mick's explanation for the purpose of his violence was not dissimilar to the young women's explanation for their self-injury—Mick was letting the "tension out", or releasing emotional pain.

These young men had experienced a variety of traumatic events, and many of them had experienced multiple traumas, but they inhabited a subcultural world where men were expected to be tough and not to display their feelings. Displays of emotion were evidence of weakness, or the antithesis of what a real man should be. Thus men internalised the emotional pain they experienced and often did not have the words to describe their feelings. This left them on edge, anxious and confused. This would simmer until it reached boiling point. One strategy for releasing pain was anger and violence. Another strategy for dealing with pain was to anaesthetise the emotions through drug and alcohol abuse, which was common and the young men articulated clearly why they used drugs. According to Andy:

> *Choof gets you stoned ... you can be happy instead of being angry all the time.*

Shawn had not used heroin for eight months when his step-grandmother died unexpectedly. Two hours later:

> *I was laughing and having fun with my friends. Smack blocks out everything and you can just forget.*

According to Matt:

> *[Drugs] numbed me, it was fun. I didn't have to think about shit.*

As Liam put it:

> *I loved alcohol ... I liked the effects ... as my anxiety became unbearable it blocked things out.*

Mick had a history of violence and unprovoked attacks on other men. However, heroin was another strategy for dealing with unpalatable emotions:

> *I loved the feeling because straight away I got a huge head rush, you forget about everything straight away.*

We can see that the young men were using drugs for a similar reason: to forget.

Conclusion

This chapter began by pointing out that the binary of men as providers and women as carers is a fundamental characteristic of working-class hegemonic masculinity. These young men assimilated this message from many sources as they were growing up. They accepted that as adult men they should be workers and providers, in much the same way that they took it for granted that men should be "tough" and not display their emotions.

However, in their teenage years it became increasingly obvious that there was no place for them in the labour force. Two-thirds (66 per cent) of the young men left school before Year 10 and another 20 per cent left at the end of Year 10 or early in Year 11. Most young people in their age group completed Year 12; the participants were simply outcompeted in the hunt for paid work. Most of them became unemployed and some eked out an existence on the margins of the labour force. Others supplemented their income with petty theft and dealing illicit drugs.

These young men could not achieve some of the main goals of working-class hegemonic masculinity: having a job, working hard, and demonstrating the potential to be a good provider, and a good partner. The failure to achieve a "respectable" place in the labour force meant they were increasingly attracted to the "wrong crowd" which celebrated working-class "machismo" and offered them a model of masculinity that was attainable to them. This value system emphasises toughness, violence, criminality and excessive drug and alcohol use. Some of the young men became leaders in this subculture, celebrating working-class machismo in all its forms. Other men were not "leaders", but they were participants in this subculture and understood its values.

There were a number of consequences to this shift from working-class hegemonic masculinity to the adoption of youthful machismo. The first was a dramatic overemphasis on male toughness and the importance of not displaying emotions, or male "weakness". The second consequence was that my participants rarely had the words to talk about their feelings. These young men had experienced many traumatic events in their lives, and much of their emotional pain had been internalised.

When the internalised pain was too difficult to bear, it led to outbursts of anger, often involving violence, and excessive drug and alcohol use designed to anaesthetise the pain. Additionally, if given the right opportunity, it prompted an unexpected outpouring of grief as we saw in Larry's case. These young men were not "bad": they were much like the young women—they carried an emotional burden too heavy to bear.

References

Australian Bureau of Statistics. (2012). *Gender indicators Australia, labour force series*. Canberra, Australia: Australian Bureau of Statistics.

Bourgois, P. (2002). *In search of respect: Selling crack in El Barrio* (2nd ed.). New York: Cambridge University Press, (e-book).

Coles, T. (2009). Negotiating the field of masculinity: The production and reproduction of multiple dominant masculinities. *Men and Masculinities, 12*(1), 30–44.

Connell, R. (2005). *Masculinities*. Cambridge: Polity Press.

De Viggiani, N. (2012). Trying to be something you area not: Masculine performances within a prison setting. *Men and Masculinities, 15*(3), 271–291.

Goffman, E. (1959). *The presentation of self in everyday life*. New York: Anchor Books.

Jewkes, Y. (2005). Men behind bars: "Doing" masculinity as an adaptation to imprisonment. *Men and Masculinities, 8*(1), 44–63.

MacDonald, R., Webster, C., Shildrick, T., & Simpson, M. (2011). Paths of exclusion, inclusion and desistance: Understanding marginalised young people's criminal careers. In S. Farrall, M. Hough, S. Maruna, & R. Sparks (Eds.), *Escape routes: Contemporary persepctives on life after punishment*. New York: Routledge.

Trimbur, L. (2011). "Tough love": Mediation and articulation in the urban boxing gym. *Ethnography, 12*(3), 334–355.

Valkonen, J., & Hänninen, V. (2012). Narratives of masculinity and depression. *Men and Masculinities, 16*(2), 160–180.

7

Moving on from Substance Abuse

When I met participants, they were all engaged in drug treatment services and working to make changes to their lives, but there were many challenges to "moving on". It is commonly suggested that change is a matter of individual will power—"If you really want to change, you will". This ascribes total agency to an individual, but also starts from the assumption that an individual seeking change has sufficient emotional resource and social capital to enact change. This individualist understanding was the approach adopted by Nancy Reagan in her infamous "Just Say No" campaign to prevent teen drug abuse in the 1980s. Despite widespread dissemination of her message, drug dependence remains a significant issue in the USA (Gray 2001; Jensen et al. 2004; Reuter 2013).

Another common narrative focuses on "recovery and redemption". The "addicted" individual hits a metaphorical "rock bottom" from which they proceed to defy all adversity and go on to "redeem" themselves. This has been the overarching narrative in a number of autobiographical books (Burroughs 2004; Ferguson 2005; Frey 2003; Holden 2005). Unfortunately, only a tiny minority of people who recover from substance abuse go on to be best-selling authors.

© The Author(s) 2016
K. Daley, *Youth and Substance Abuse*,
DOI 10.1007/978-3-319-33675-6_7

There are diverse treatment options for people experiencing substance abuse, and all point out that problematic substance use is not simply a "free choice". For example, proponents of the "disease" model of addiction contend that the individual has very little control of their behaviour because of neurological adaption, whereas various 12-step models (Alcoholics Anonymous, Narcotics Anonymous etc.) believe that individuals are at the mercy of a "higher power" (Alcoholics Anonymous 2005). And those who subscribe to a social-ecological model of health contend that drug abuse is but one factor of a constellation of bio-psycho-social factors at play in an individual's life. The model draws from the Ottawa Charter of health promotion (World Health Organisation 1986).

Bruun and Mitchell (2012) have developed a therapeutic practice framework for youth alcohol and other drug services. Instead of proposing a single approach, they suggest that young people should be understood within evidence-based theories of development and with attention to risk chains and protective factors in a person's life. Drawing from clinical literature and an action-research project with senior clinicians, Bruun and Mitchell (2012) propose ten characteristics of effective youth AOD treatments. Good programs/services will be:

1. Client centred/socio-culturally relevant
2. Relationship based
3. Developmentally appropriate
4. Comprehensive, holistic, ecological, multi-systemic and integrative
5. Family focused
6. Of sufficient duration and intensity
7. Adopting sound engagement and retention strategies
8. Behavioural, experiential and skill focused
9. Building on strengths
10. Use theory and evidence to guide program design and refinement

(Bruun and Mitchell 2012, p. 7)

These characteristics are similar to the principles of the Adolescent Community Reinforcement Approach (A-CRA) used widely in the USA when working with young people experiencing problematic substance use (Godley et al. 2001). A-CRA maintains that having the family involved in treatment, fostering "pro-social" activities that do not involve drug use and ensuring positive reinforcement in all aspects of a young person's life are fundamental to successful pathways out of substance use.

In the UK, and increasingly in Australia, the concept of *recovery capital* has been a focus (Best and Laudet n.d.). Recovery capital refers to the amount of resources an individual has to draw upon in their pathway to recovery from substance abuse. Cloud and Granfield (2009) describe recovery capital as comprising four domains in an individual's life: (1) social capital, (2) human capital, (3) physical capital, and (4) cultural capital. These domains seek to identify the resources an individual has available to them. It is hypothesised that those with greater resources and lower drug use severity are more suited to brief interventions, whereas those with few resources and greater severity require longer-term, more intensive supports.

All of these approaches to guiding effective interventions for people experiencing problem substance use have two key principles: (1) they frame substance use as one aspect of an individual's life; and (2) they understand that effective change is made more or less difficult by factors which extend beyond the individual's control.

This chapter begins by outlining how individuals identified their respective "tipping points" for changing their drug use. Then the chapter examines three types of treatment available to young people in Victoria. After that, the young people's aspirations for the future are described. The chapter shows that "moving on" is not easy for those with little recovery capital.

Tipping Points

For many young people, the transition from recreational drug use to a substance abuse problem happened slowly. The usual order of events was that drug use began with alcohol and cannabis, but it was several years before other drugs entered the mix. For most of the participants, their physical dependency on drugs came as a surprise. Jakey said:

> I stayed at a mate's house and I didn't take any choof because I wasn't that hardcore—well, I didn't think I was. Then I couldn't sleep for two days and then I figured it out because I was going crazy and had to go home to get choof—that's when I knew I was addicted.

Jakey had developed a physical dependency well before he realised it.

Chris was resistant to the suggestion that his drug use was a problem because he was in full-time employment. He compared himself to his friends who were unemployed and using. "I thought, 'I work full-time doing my apprenticeship and I smoke just as much as you' as though I was some sort of sick cunt! [laughing]." Chris explained that managing heavy use as well as employment became increasingly difficult. Struggling to wake up in the morning, he found that his day continued with an enormous effort:

> *I had been lying to myself that I had this energy ... I dragged myself out of bed, had a shower, if I could even be bothered doing that. Then the whole way to work ... I would just sit there thinking about how not to go to work. "Just turn around, call in sick, quit your job if you have to." And then the other voice in my head is, "Nah, you've got to work, you've got to do this for five more years, you can't call in sick today". I'd do that all day.*

Eventually, he realised that his drug use was severely interfering with his ability to keep his employment—not only was he physically dependent, but he was also depressed. When I interviewed him, he was undergoing a two-week residential withdrawal program.

Pailin also found that dependency crept up on him:

> *At first, using was only for fun, for friends ... I didn't notice that I got hooked— that's when I needed it every day. It's a need now; it's not a want anymore. I don't want to get stoned; I do it because I need it. If I don't, I'll feel really sick.*

The realisation that drug use was no longer pleasurable was a common sentiment. Will spelled out this conundrum in more detail:

> *I am not happy when I have got it—it's hard to explain. I love getting smashed, but it doesn't make me happy. I will be sitting there stoned out and I will be like, "I need another cone", and even if I went and got a cone, I wouldn't be happy ... When I am smashed I think to myself, "You know what? This isn't that good—what's the difference between this and sober?" It doesn't make me happy. But when I am sober, it's like all I am doing is chasing it. I can't help it.*

Will's confusion as to why he was "chasing it" illustrated the complexity of understanding dependency. He clearly had a strong psychological desire to stop. Yet his experience of physical withdrawal meant that when he was substance-free, his body's desire for the drug drove his want for more, despite it not providing him with pleasure.

For some young women, participating in criminal activity was the point at which it was clear to them that their drug use was a problem. When asked when she felt her drug use was getting out of hand, Ashly was clear: "When we started robbing for it." Ebony's answer was similar:

It started when I was 13, I just had an occasional habit. When I started working for it—selling myself—then I was thinking, "Whoa, okay" ... Then the first time I worked I didn't want to do it ... I started selling myself, just buying drugs, taking heroin.

Jahl had only started to consider his drug use a problem a few months before I met him:

I was all over the place. I realised that choof was ruling my life. If you'd asked me five months ago, I'd have said, "Yeah, I am gonna keep smoking, I am loving life!", but now, no more.

He explained that living on the streets saw him witness a dark underbelly of society, including experiences that he would carry with him for life. These experiences were the impetus for his wanting to change:

I realised, "You can't live here" ... after three months I got out of there. That's why I am getting off the choof now—I am trying to get my life together.

Jahl also had an alternate activity—running—which he gained much from and which was being compromised by his drug use. He had a natural talent which had attracted the eye of a successful athletics coach. Jahl's enjoyment in the sport, and the sense of achievement from success, saw his desire to use drugs dissipate. He had found a social activity where he felt a sense of belonging and it did not involve drugs. What we see here is an increase in what clinicians refer to as "pro-social activity". The premise of some methods of working with young offenders is not to focus on changing a "problem" behaviour but to instead increase the availability and opportunity of behaviours that are positive and personally enjoyable for the youth. Connecting a young person with positive activities is seen to reduce the likelihood that they will engage in risky behaviour, while giving them greater connection to protective factors such as community and peers.

In contrast, Jakey's drug use had gotten to the point where it had isolated him from any social activity and this had affected his psychosocial well-being. This realisation was his impetus for change:

> *I have one friend and I used to have a million friends ... I can't even talk to people. If I am stoned, I can't look people in the eye because I am too self-conscious about the way I sound and how I look. I just feel like I am a dirty drug addict ... I am not worth talking to when I get stoned ... if we were sitting here [stoned] now I would not be able to think about anything to say to you ... it's like I get trapped in my own head.*

Jakey's description of feeling like a "dirty drug addict" tapped into a theme which emerged in many of the interviews: that once one had developed a drug problem, there was a point of no return. This was not defined by physical or psychological dependence but by the concept of one being a "junkie" or an "addict". The "junkie" is a socially constructed concept. For many, it was defined solely by injecting drug use—once someone injected drugs, they had crossed a clear line.

For those who did inject, a "junkie" was often defined more narrowly. Some felt that one only becomes a "junkie" if one undertook sex work or crime to support your habit. Those who did engage in sex work reported that this was a lesser evil than other crime. Young people all had an idea of what a "junkie" was, but their definitions varied. A "junkie" was always a deeply stigmatised identity.

Jessica was frightened of becoming a "junkie". She was unusual because she made the call to a drug treatment service of her own volition after her brother, who was previously a client, gave her the details of the youth withdrawal unit.

I felt like if I didn't fix my life then I was never going to be anyone, and I'd either end up a junkie, or kill myself or something. So I felt like I had to do it … when you feel really shit you get desperate … [drug use] wasn't working for me anymore. I'd sit there, and my dad would be smacked off his face [on heroin], and I'd just sit there so angry and jealous, and that's not the way I want to live my life—I don't want to be like that.

Stacey was also frightened of becoming an "addict". She explained that she was out scoring with her friends one day and saw them all use needles:

We were sitting in the toilets doing all their things with their needles and one of them said to me, "This could be you," she was saying. "Do you wanna use a needle?" And I got pretty scared by it and I called up this place [detox] and was like, "I need help".

For several of the young women a failed suicide attempt was a tipping point in their lives. Mary said:

When I was in hospital [psychiatric], I sort of decided that the life I was living wasn't really a life, and if I am going to make the choice to be alive—which is every second that I am living—then there is obviously no point in trying to destroy my brain. I might as well be dead if I am doing that. So I guess that's my motivation. I don't really enjoy being sober or pushing myself to do all these things, but it's gotten less unbearable, so I guess that motivates me to keep going.

She expressed what all of the young women who had attempted suicide spoke of. They had not wanted to die but felt unable to live. Suicide as a motivator to change was only reported by young women.

Another experience exclusive to the women was that ending drug use was a positive consequence of leaving a toxic relationship. Lisa had wanted to escape both her violent relationship, as well as the drug use:

We were doing it all the time … I just wanted to get away from the drugs. [Wanting to leave my relationship] just pushed me even more to sort my life out and get off the drugs. I don't think you can have a relationship with someone when they use drugs a lot, because it's just always fighting or anger.

Lisa's partner's violence towards her was extreme. In one incident, he beat her on a busy corner in the inner-city while people stood by and watched. As her head hit the concrete she heard her skull crack. She lost consciousness and woke up in intensive care.

There is no magic formula for when young people decide to change their drug use. For some it is relatively early in their drug-using "career"; for others it is much later; for some it involves multiple false starts; and for some the "dance with death" is final.

Interventions

Participants entered drug treatment services in a variety of ways. For a lot of the young people, formal interventions were a seemingly fortuitous opportunity. Rarely were interventions sought out, mostly because young people did not know that services were available to them. Many of the men and some of the women were first referred by the courts. For a lot of young people, an initial recalcitrance about initiating contact delayed access to treatment for some time.

Participants often felt that they had "chosen" to use drugs. Thus, it was their problem and they should deal with it themselves. For example, Stacey said: "I try dealing with stuff on my own, because I don't like to ask people for help." Similarly, Jazmine also avoided seeking out assistance:

> I am not proud in the sense that I care about how I look like or anything; I am just very independent. I don't like help which is stupid. I should get rid of that because everyone needs help.

The boys were equally reluctant to initiate contact with a treatment service and were mostly referred through the court. There is certainly a connection between drug use and crime, which makes using the justice system as a vehicle for treatment logical. But there is not a strong case to be made for what, precisely, the relationship between the two factors is (Newburn 1999). The high number of young men who had been referred via the court demonstrates that the diversionary method may work; however, it is unknown how many young men without criminal histories are facing serious AOD issues.

Of the 35 young men, 24 had had contact with the youth justice system, and it was often through this that they were first referred to services for their drug use. This was typically as part of a diversionary order, so while treatment was "voluntary", it was a "choice" between a harsh punishment and a less harsh one. Consequently, engagement with the treatment system was often met with ambivalence.

However, when young people engaged with the services, misleading ideas about what "drug treatment" entailed were typically dispelled. Few of the young people interviewed were still required to be engaged in treatment. For the most part, they had chosen to continue working with the service as a voluntary client after their mandated period ended. James was referred by his lawyer to "look good in court", acknowledging that once he started seeing a worker, "I realised that I actually do have a problem".

In the interviews, many of the young people reported that being "forced" into an AOD service had actually been of great benefit to them. Matty's tipping point came about after involvement with the youth justice system. The court required that he access an AOD service, as well as placing him on a youth supervision order. In retrospect, he identified both actions as important agents for change:

> I am glad that I got the order and I am still out here [rather than incarcerated], because I would probably be a lot worse.

Simon, too, had come into contact with the justice system and was now certain that he would not re-offend. He had been on a good-behaviour bond, but was uncertain if it had expired yet or not. He was indifferent about whether he was still on the order because he was adamant that he was "not going to get in any other trouble anyway". Likewise, Amy was certain that she would not re-offend:

> I was on a five-year good-behaviour bond, and then I was on a separate six-month one. I think I am off it now. I don't get into trouble any more—last time I went to court it scared the shit out of me … If I wasn't pregnant they would have thrown me in gaol but that got me out of it—thank God. I don't want to go down that path again.

There are three modes of treatment available to young people in Victoria: outreach programs, residential withdrawal programs ("detox"), and youth residential rehabilitation services ("therapeutic communities" or "rehab"). These are described next.

Outreach Programs

Outreach is the primary mode of treatment in Victoria. Outreach workers go out to find and meet clients and pro-actively seek to engage them. Workers have access to cars and flexibility in their day's structure so as to be able to meet the needs of the young people they work with. Given young people's hesitations in contacting services themselves, having outreach as the key service modality makes sense.

In Victoria, youth AOD services started in 1998. In the mid-1990s there was a heroin glut in Melbourne which saw cheap, high-quality heroin readily available. There was increased street trade, visible public use of heroin, and the number of fatal overdoses increased dramatically (Rowe 2002). There was a public outcry, and the state government commissioned an inquiry into the issue, known as *The Pennington Report* (Victorian Premier's Drug Advisory Council 1996).

One of the report's key findings was that there were no youth-specific AOD services. This finding received considerable media attention, and the "Kids at Risk" headlines led to a swift response from the Victorian government. Funding was provided for a youth-specific residential withdrawal service, as well as youth outreach workers.

Tasked with identifying clients, outreach workers focused on finding visible drug users on the streets. The outreach approach had continued because of its efficacy at being able to engage with clients who do not attend office-based appointments. This is often those who are the most marginalised or who struggle to engage with more structured models of interventions (Forrell and Gray 2009; Priebe and Matanov n.d.; St Christopher House 2007).

Outreach allows the client to work closely with the same worker for as long as they need. This provides a therapeutic relationship which can be practically oriented (i.e. assisting with physical needs—health, housing, withdrawal), or psychologically oriented (counselling, self-development).

For marginalised young people, their outreach worker is often their only "safe" adult figure. Not surprisingly, this relationship can be of much benefit to them (Ungar 2013). There is yet to be an established, evidence-based model for the approach used in an outreach setting and the outcomes of outreach as a form of intervention with this population have not been systematically evaluated. Common sense would suggest that this model would be more effective than an office-based method given the population are often not voluntary clients, most of whom are homeless. The participants in the study almost universally had positive reflections on their experiences of outreach.

Alex lived in a home where she received very little support or encouragement. She explained that it was great when she started work with an outreach worker as she felt "more comfortable with my worker—I can open myself up a bit more".

For Maddison, an outreach worker was the first person to validate her feelings about the abuse that was happening at home. Maddison had been seeking psychological support at school. She had seen her school counsellor and talked to her about some of the things that were going on at home. However, the counsellor did not "have any advice and didn't investigate further". Maddison concluded that "my problem mustn't have been as bad as I thought it was". Once she had a worker she was able to receive "legitimation" of her emotions from a professional.

James described how he found having an outreach worker:

It's a good means of support—it helps a lot. It helps you set goals; it helps me to look at stuff—my drug use and my issues.

Roxanne had been homeless since she was very young and was still grieving the deaths of her friends and grandfather. She had not previously thought about the potential links between these deaths, her homelessness and her risk-taking behaviour:

YSAS has helped me so much in realising why I do things; that I am not just an idiot, but that I do things for a reason. Everyone does things for a reason. And sometimes when you're down and out, you just need someone to tell you that you're not a freak, that you are a human, and that you're dealing with things okay.

Roxanne's outreach worker was able to help her make the links between her trauma and her drug use, while also validating her pain and promoting her self-worth. Ungar (2013) has concluded that it is beneficial for all young people to have positive relationships with adults, but the benefits are particularly significant for marginalised young people who have no family support.

Residential Withdrawal Programs ("Detox")

Withdrawal stays are up to two weeks long, and the withdrawal units resemble a house rather than a hospital, providing food, safety, medical services and other care often not available to marginalised youth. There are seven youth residential withdrawal units in Victoria and there is usually a waiting list to get in.

Some people had stumbled across residential withdrawal accidentally. Roxanne had a friend who was accessing a residential withdrawal unit:

I went to visit him, and they were talking to me and said I should go in, and I did, and that was probably the best thing I ever did for myself.

Roxanne found there were both practical and psychological benefits from her stay in a withdrawal unit:

It gives you a bit of a break and it gives you a bit to think more clearly about things that you couldn't really think about when you've got to worry about money and a house.

In the course of undertaking the fieldwork, it became apparent that those who were homeless benefitted from detox in ways that were not formal measures of success. For instance, putting on weight or getting on top of transport fines were tasks that seemed simple but were essentially impossible to achieve while they were homeless. This group may well have higher relapse rates, but that is likely to be proportionate to their higher needs.

Simon was in a withdrawal unit when I interviewed him. He explained that he had often spoken about quitting drugs but never managed to remain abstinent for more than a couple of days. The intense dreaming—which is common with cannabis withdrawal—was too difficult to bear. His decision to make a more permanent change married up with his new goals for the future that required controlling his drug use:

> *The main reason that I am here is so that I can achieve being able to get up every morning and go to work. I want to start my first year apprenticeship.*

Kate was also in a withdrawal unit when I met her. She had been there several times before but this time she was determined to succeed. Previously, she had been unable to get past the third day. When I met her, she had been in the detox for a week and was planning to stay for another week:

> *The way I am thinking of it at the moment is that as boring as I might find it in here, when I get out, it's probably going to be just as boring. Sure, I can get into drugs or alcohol or whatever, but at the moment it's better for me to be here.*

In the course of the fieldwork it became apparent that many of the young people had come into contact with services through some opportune happenstance. I wondered how many young people would benefit from these services but were unaware of their existence. This was particularly an area of concern for the young women who were less likely to appear before a magistrate and, in turn, be referred to drug treatment services.

Lisa first stumbled into a YSAS drop-in centre when her boyfriend told her about a place they could go to get food. Later, her mother found the details of a youth residential withdrawal service. Lisa was relieved to see that it was also run by the same people that gave her the food: "I would probably still be on heroin now if I didn't find this place."

Lisa had been in the withdrawal unit twice. The first time she withdrew from heroin and was placed onto a pharmacotherapy. This time she was withdrawing from the pharmacotherapy. I asked her if she missed using:

> *Not really; sometimes. But then I think about the consequences and I don't want to get sick anymore. I really want to start putting on weight again—just be healthier.*

The young person's readiness for change was a strong factor in the outcomes of their stay in a withdrawal unit. Jake had recently broken up with his girlfriend and was evaluating many aspects of his life:

> *The break up put me in this place. [After the break up] I was like, "Fuck this" … I just hammered it and I was going five days out of the week for a few months—eckies and speed and ice, but speed predominantly … I hadn't slept in four days and I called here [residential withdrawal] and they were like, "Come in and do an assessment". … then I got a short-notice call up three days before I came in so I just said, "Yep".*

It was fortunate that Jake was able to get a place in a withdrawal unit so quickly. This capitalised on his momentum for change following the end of his relationship with his girlfriend. Jake was ready to take action immediately.

For the young men especially, peer groups and social connectedness were an area of their lives which they generally did not want to step away from. However, when young people were able to distance themselves from their peers, changes to their drug use were usually more successful. Jake was separated from his peers by accident:

> *A few weeks ago the phone company cut off my phone and that was probably the best thing that could have happened to me because the last three weeks I haven't had any contact with the guys I was doing drugs with—I was away from the stuff, so that was good for me.*

When I met Jake, he had been substance-free for well over a month and had much clarity about his immediate future. He was hoping to move onto a three-month residential rehabilitation program after his stay in the withdrawal unit: "I don't trust myself … [two weeks in the detox] is not enough. It's a temporary stint. It's not enough to break a cycle and a habit."

Youth Residential Rehabilitation Models ("Rehab")

Youth residential rehabilitation models in Victoria draw from the principles of a "therapeutic community". Rather than the traditional 28-day hospital-style stay, young people go and live on a property for up to six months and are able to work through their issues in a safe, secure environment. Trained staff understand the physical and emotional needs of the participants and undertake care-planning on an individual basis. The key focus of the program is on maintaining abstinence, group work, recreational activities and improving physical and mental health.

Pailin realised he needed an extended period of time away from his daily environment to break the psychological aspects of his dependence and address the reasons why he used drugs so heavily. Six months in a youth therapeutic community allowed him to do this. He transitioned from the residential rehabilitation to a supported accommodation program and was abstinent for more than two years. Unfortunately, he began using again following a personal crisis. He was in "detox" when I interviewed him.

Shawn, the young man whose infant brother died in the car, had remained abstinent for some months after completing a residential rehabilitation program. Undertaking this radical change was a massive commitment:

> I gave up every friend I ever had—I don't speak to anyone. I've moved to the opposite side of the city, I have changed my number and I don't see anyone that I used to. I am trying to make new friends.

Giving up all of your friends when you are, for the most part, without any family support is an almost impossible task in the longer term. Shawn was gay and felt that the most common social thing other young gay men did was to party together—a scene he was trying to avoid. Shawn was struggling to make friends in a new city, far from where he had grown up. It remained to be seen if his radical isolation would be sustainable.

When I met Damian, he had not had a drink in eight months, nor smoked cannabis in the previous four. He was, quite rightly, very proud. He explained that he had been in environments with heavy drug use and still managed to abstain. Damian's motivation to get out of this cycle was clear:

> My mum and dad, the way they are is because they didn't deal with stuff when they were young, so I am not going to do the same. They didn't deal with their stuff and it all came out in the divorce, and it tended to ricochet off onto us

kids. I have lived my life not wanting that to happen to someone else. If I have kids down the track, I don't want that to happen to them.

Damian still had a lot to manage in his life. He had serious decisions to make about his physical health, one of which involved major surgery. The prospect of this had previously seemed unfathomable to him, but as time had passed, he had established strengths and resources which had made him feel that it was a possibility. After Damien left rehab, he had maintained contact with his outreach worker who was an "anchor point" in his life.

Moving On?

By the time I met them, all of the young people were attempting to move on from substance abuse. However, it is important to remember that we are not dealing with a homogeneous group. The young people did have two things in common: they had come to the realisation that they had a substance abuse problem, and they had undergone physical withdrawal from drugs and/or alcohol. Nonetheless, they were not all the same. Next, I discuss factors that were likely to affect their chances of rebuilding their lives.

First of all, some of the young people had only relatively short periods of abstinence under their belts whereas others had notched up many months of sobriety. Those who had achieved a sustained period of being "clean and sober" had usually made more steps towards rebuilding their lives and had greater self-confidence. On the other hand, some had previously achieved a sustained period of abstinence only to relapse when confronted by some major disappointment or personal crisis in their lives. Length of sobriety is an important factor but relapses are still fairly common.

The young people also had different goals with regard to their drug and alcohol use. For most their goal was total abstinence, but for a minority the goal in the longer term was a substantial reduction in consumption. They wanted "more control" and to return to recreational use like many other young people.

The young people varied in their maturity and world experience. The youngest person in the study was only 14, whereas others were in their late teens and some were in their early 20s. There was variation in their family circumstance. For a small number there was the possibility of returning to live with a parent, but most were disconnected from family, and some had no parents to return to. The lack of a "home" to return to, or a family who would support them, left these young people very vulnerable. Finally, there was variation in their level of educational achievement and in their experience of paid work. All of these factors are likely to affect their chances of rebuilding their lives.

Learning from Experience

Bearing the above factors in mind, it is not surprising that people learn from experience in different ways and at different speeds. Moreover, some lessons have to be taught more than once. Jazmine knew that she had had a troubled childhood and that she had made some bad decisions during her adolescent years. She said, "I am well aware that there was a problem and that I took drugs to block it all out and then I created another problem." Jazmine had made an important step forward, in that she now understood the function of her drug use. This was critical to her being ready to shape her life in a positive direction.

In contrast, Luke appeared to have a long journey ahead of him. When I met Luke his sense of self-worth was low:

> I just feel like everything's stuffed up for me from drugs—I've just lost so many friends and everything. Even they said that I am getting in too far over my head. I got to that point, and I still remember it; I wanted to catch up with them, and they just didn't want to see me or what I was turning out like, because they could see what I was doing and they felt sorry for me. ... they didn't really want to hang out anymore because I was changing so much ... I was always lying to everyone.

Luke felt isolated and unloved. During the interview he began to talk about his parents' separation and the subsequent acrimony that followed between different members of the family. At the time, his mother and his siblings received counselling, but he declared that he was "fine" and did not want to talk about it. In retrospect, it seems likely that his parents' separation had affected him deeply even though he was only dimly aware of this at the time. His drug use began soon after his father left the family home and this was probably his way of coping with the emotional turmoil in his head.

Jessica was further along the road to recovery than Luke. She accepted responsibility for her drug use, but at the same time she could identify external factors that limited her choices:

> *I always say that I made a lot of decisions: I decided to leave school; I decided to start doing drugs. I don't blame my parents for the way that I am; but I know that at the same time, I wouldn't be the way that I am without them making a lot of bad decisions.*

She accepted that she had made some bad choices, but this was empowering her to feel that she could make choices—including good ones. She acknowledged that she had faced disadvantages beyond her control: her parents had made a lot of bad decisions that affected her. Nonetheless, her ability to take responsibility for her decisions meant that she did not express the same level of guilt and apparent self-loathing that Luke did.

Amber was now seeking to slowly withdraw from her pharmacotherapy as she prepared for the arrival of her first child. She had accepted the gravity of her past, as well as her ability to make the most of her own future:

> *I used to break down and cry and all that [talking about this stuff], and now I am trying to get over the past—which you have to do. You can't keep the past with you your whole life. You have to get over it! And since I have been learning to get over it, I have been smiling more!*

Another person who had made significant strides on her journey towards recovery was Lizzie. Following a stay in "rehab", she had been off of drugs for 102 days when I met her. This was her longest period of abstinence with the exception of when she had been incarcerated. This time, however, the decision to not use drugs had been entirely her own. Lizzie's goals were written out and kept in a folder that she had with her:

> Do the social work degree. Continue staying clean. Keep doing the 12 steps of NA. Getting my driver's licence is on there, but I have done that ... a few goals for things around my house ... get a job in a month or two. Improve my memory. Improve my English skills. Join a gym—which I did. ... Continue to be involved with the charity that I am involved with ... I want to get the most out of my life. I want to be healthy, and be a social worker, and help people. I want to have a family one day.

Lizzie's headspace was positive. She had permanent accommodation in community housing and was rebuilding her life.

As a way of fostering reflection, participants were asked what advice they would give to a younger version of themselves. Many laughed that they did not think they would listen to someone else's advice at that age. Nonetheless, their responses to this question gave an insight into what they may have benefited from and what they had learned.

Jai, whose mother had died of a heroin overdose when he was in primary school, said:

> Try not to be naive. You'll make all the choices that you make, they'll become you. And hopefully you'll make the right choices and don't be down on yourself if you don't, 'cause you'll still get through life no matter how you do it, just look after yourself, and keep your health with you and your brain with you and you'll be fine.

Mick was concerned his little brother was going to follow the same path as he had:

> That's just the one thing I don't want to see: for him to turn out exactly like me. If he turns out exactly like me he's got a whole lot of shit ahead of him.

Likewise, Shawn, who was gay, wanted for his younger brother to have a different life. Shawn's concern about what his brother might see if he follows in his footsteps gives some insight into what Shawn has witnessed and experienced in his own lifetime.

My brother is about to turn 13—the age I was when I started using [heroin]—and he's now just starting to go through stuff and I don't want that. I don't want to live like that anymore. I don't want him to have a life like that—I've watched it completely ruin my family.

Amy's advice was brief: "Make your own decisions in life—don't let anyone tell you what to do. But don't give up." Ebony's also showed this "never give up" attitude:

Just keep at it. Don't kill yourself—'cause it's not worth it. Just get support; stop doing stuff on your own—trying to give up [drugs] on your own. Get some balls and go and talk to people.

Asking participants to offer these reflections on their own pathways was fruitful. These young people very articulately captured why they feel they had developed a drug problem. When I asked Roxanne if there was "anything else that is important?", she replied:

I have always felt like an outsider, that I've never fitted in. And I am always having to pretend that I am happy when I am not, and pretend that everything's okay when it's not ... I never thought I'd end up a heroin addict ... but if you keep getting beaten down ... there's a certain point where it gets too much.

This research sought to answer why some young people came to experience problematic substance use. Roxanne had provided an important insight.

The Future

When asked about their plans for the future, none of the young people had grandiose aspirations. Most participants had goals similar to Stacey's, who just wanted to "live a normal nine-to-five life". People often used the phrase a "normal life". By this they meant such things as a house, a job, a partner and a family. However, we will see later that there were differences in the aspirations of men and women. Both sexes endorsed a traditional division of labour between men and women—that of "home-maker" and "breadwinner".

The first priority for people who had only recently come out of detox was to maintain their sobriety and find stable housing. According to Riley, her goals for the immediate future were:

> Getting my drug use down, and my housing sorted, and just trying to cope with things—it's really hard ... I think, because I hadn't dealt with a lot of my family issues, it all came out and I started seeing a psychologist ... then it was like, "Oh, I've got to deal with all of this stuff".

Those who were still homeless were usually unable to plan ahead. When asked her goals, Mary replied:

> To survive ... I don't really know. I don't have any definite plans for my future, but I guess, to cut down on drugs as much as I can and eventually be able to work.

Time in withdrawal units was often dedicated to finding a bed in a refuge or other housing arrangements when they left, but if these young people were unsuccessful, then they were acutely at risk once they were on their own. Sleeping on the street stoned was much more bearable than to be sober.

Some young people had found stable accommodation. Ebony was living in a Christian boarding house at the time I interviewed her. There was a strict "no sex, drugs, smoking, alcohol" policy, which suited Ebony, who was committed to remaining "clean and sober". Her single room was very modest, but it was stable and this provided her with a sense of "home".

Maddison was living with her father, but this was problematic because she was convinced that he did not care for her. This was made clear to Maddison when she had an operation on her hand. Her doctor had told her not to wash the dishes, but her father expected her to do them when he felt too tired. He was also controlling: "I have to keep all of my food containers in my room because he thinks my stuff takes up too much space in the kitchen." He was also mean: "He told me I go to the toilet a lot, so I should get my own toilet paper." Maddison might have been "at home" but there was no love in this house.

In terms of "getting out" of their current lifestyle, women were likely to see education and training as essential, whereas the young men rarely spoke of this. Men were much more likely to be looking for employment.

Table 4.1 showed that 61 per cent of the young people had left school by the end of Year 9, another 24 per cent left at the end of Year 10 and only 12 per cent completed their high school certificate (Year 12). Not only was this problematic for their own development, but they were part of a generation where more than 80 per cent of their peers completed secondary education. Not having a high school certificate was a major barrier to finding employment.

Many of the young women (and a small number of men) expressed a desire to work in the helping professions—aged care, youth work, social work. Often, this was because a good worker had helped them change their lives and they wanted to help others in similar circumstances to themselves. They needed formal qualifications to work in these professions. Many participants, usually women, had started vocational courses provided through TAFE.

Jess had completed many certificates in various welfare skills—aged care, community care, disability support—yet the criminal record she received after intervening into a fight her father had with the police precluded her from working in most of these professions.

Maddison and Maggie had also left school after the end of Year 11 and completed a certificate in aged care. Maddison subsequently got a job in a nursing home which she really enjoyed. Maddison was beginning to rebuild her life. She was studying at TAFE with the long-term goals of working in nutrition and owning her own home. Her determination shone through. This was similar to Maggie, who was now studying nursing part-time and feeling positive about her future.

While several of the young people had completed further study—often accumulating many certificates—there did not appear to be a strong link between these and successful employment. Some women did gain employment in the same field as their vocational study, but most did not. Those who did were almost universally in aged care, which in Victoria is desperately under-staffed.

Apart from aged care courses, the other certificates young people had completed were often unlikely to benefit their career prospects. Often the skills learnt in these courses were so specific that they were not very transferable. Thus, the benefits of training were often not felt by these young people. This affected the women more than men, as the women were more likely to be seeking an exit through education and training.

Some of the young women had found casual employment as a consequence of their training. We saw above that Maddison was working in aged care, but this was a casual job, not a permanent position. We also met Maggie earlier. She was working in a nursing home while she studied nursing, but her employment was also casual. One young woman, Stacey, was undertaking an apprenticeship as a chef, which was likely to lead to a permanent job, but this was unusual. All of those who had gained employment were precariously employed. MacDonald et al. (2005) report similar findings. They challenge the oft-held view that marginalised youth are permanently unemployed and instead explain that gaining employment was achieved often, though maintaining work was the far greater issue.

Despite the young women often beginning or planning to undertake further training and education, their longer-term goals largely did not involve work. Many of the women seemed to expect—or perhaps accept—that their future roles would be as stay-at-home mothers. For many of the women, the role of work was a peripheral part of their discussions of the future—none of the women spoke about needing to work as a way of supporting a family. Despite the fact that many of these women had been raised by single mothers, very few of them approached adulthood with a notion that they would, or could, be financially independent. There was an implicit assumption that they would have a partner who would be the main breadwinner.

Equally as traditional in their gender role expectations were the young men. Their desire to enter employment as soon as possible was closely tied to their belief that a "man" should provide for his family. When asked about their futures, the men's answers were remarkably similar. Andrew wanted: "to have a house to live in, to have a good job and a girlfriend". Likewise, Asiah said: "I just want to get a job and to get some money. Hopefully in a few years' time I will have a family." Michael was also sure and succinct: "I want to have a job one day. I want to get married. I want to have kids." Nearly all of the young men, except for Shawn,

Jai and Liam, who were gay, wanted to get married and expected to be the main breadwinner.

The women made little reference to the need to earn money, but this dominated the men's narratives of their future goals. Will, for example, said:

> *I have to get off drugs so that I can start saving for a car, save for the repayments on a house. You have to have a good source of income for even the deposit.*

Beau had similar goals: "To have a job, to get a nice house. Just the basics."

For the young men, the ability to be a provider was often tied to their idea of being an adequate suitor. Andy wanted to "get a job, get a house" so that he could then "get a missus and settle down". For Michael, earning money was central to being a worthy partner:

> *You need to show her that you have money to spend on her and that you actually come from a good family.*

The men were clear: they wanted a job, a home and a wife.

The (heterosexual) young men were mainly working class and their aspirations for employment were wedded to their belief that a man is a "worker". In contrast to the young women, about one-quarter of the young men had at some point participated in the work force, before their drug and alcohol use had burgeoned out of control. Most of their experience had been in blue-collar work.

Ben, for instance, left school at the beginning of Year 9 but found employment in landscape gardening shortly afterwards. Likewise, Simon was able to pick up work as a casual labourer with a friend—he'd "just call him up and he'd find stuff for me to do". Brandon left school at the end of Year 10. Eventually, he gained employment, first in rooftiling, then carpentry and then cabinet making. At the time of the interview, Brandon was homeless and unemployed. He was hoping to get work picking fruit.

There was a similar series of events for Chris, who left school at the beginning of Year 12. After a few months of "bludging", he began an apprenticeship in painting and decorating. He described the satisfaction he got from paid work:

It's good. It does a number on your body, but it's good. You begin each day and you get something done.

Jakey, who had just turned 20, left school in Year 11 and moved through various jobs. First he worked a call centre and then bricklaying. He had not worked for a year at the time of the interview. He had spent the previous 12 months "sitting in my room smoking dope, unfortunately".

Few of the men spoke about careers or the desire to work for its own pleasure. There were some exceptions. Pupps wanted to be a writer and Jerry had recently completed a course to work in real estate. Jerry had a job arranged with a real estate agent; however, Jerry said that the real estate industry was at its lowest point in a decade and he was worried that this was not a good time to start.

As we have seen, most of the men wanted blue-collar work. James eloquently summarised the views of the majority:

I want to be a tradie or something like that. I don't really have too many high hopes, but I want to … make money.

Gerald defined his future success by the ability to earn a wage:

I don't want to be a fucking dead-beat on the dole for the rest of my life. I want to make good money. I am not really into the materialistic way of thinking, but I do still want to have my own home.

Gerald had left school during Year 7 with no formal qualifications but he knew what he aspired to:

My mate, he's got a trade, he's paying off a house, he's got a girlfriend—he's living the dream pretty much.

For these young men their "dream" was a job, a house, a girlfriend (or wife) and, later, children. How many of them will achieve their dreams is unknown, but their chances in the labour market are not good.

Conclusion

This chapter began at the point where participants realised that their own drug use had become a problem, and it identified the "tipping point" when they realised that the negative effects of substance abuse outweighed the positives. This had led them, in a variety of ways, to drug treatment services. The three main drug treatment options in Victoria were described: outreach programs, residential withdrawal programs, and youth residential rehabilitation models. It was pointed out that court-mandated treatment appeared to have been effective in getting these young people into treatment, as too were diversionary orders and non-custodial sentences; however, these methods of referral meant few women were being referred.

All of the young people were attempting to remain "clean and sober", but they varied in their maturity and world experience. The youngest person in the study was only 14, whereas others were in their late teens and some were in their early 20s. There was also variation in their family circumstance with only a small number having the possibility of returning to live with parents. Furthermore, there was variation in their level of educational achievement and in their experience of paid work. All of these factors come into the mix when young people are attempting to rebuild their lives. Bearing this in mind, it is not surprising that some young people were making better progress than others.

All of the young people were working towards a life free from problematic drug use and to live what they termed a "normal life". To do this, there were two main routes: education or employment. Women were far more likely to be undertaking additional education. However, most had enrolled in vocational education which rarely led to a vocation. Young men aspired to enter the workforce and most of them were looking for blue-collar work. However, given their educational background and their lack of work experience, their prospects in the labour market were bleak.

These young men and women had begun to take the first steps towards sobriety and abstinence, but for all of them there was a long journey ahead.

References

Alcoholics Anonymous. (2005). *Twelve steps and twelve traditions*. New York: Alcoholics Anonymous World Services.

Best, D., & Laudet, A. B. (n.d.). *The potential of recovery capital*. Retrieved February 26, 2014, from http://www.thersa.org/__data/assets/pdf_file/0006/328623/A4-recovery-capital-230710-v5.pdf

Bruun, A., & Mitchell, P. (2012). *A resource for strengthening therapeutic practice frameworks in youth AOD services*. Melbourne: Youth Support and Advocacy Service.

Burroughs, A. (2004). *Dry: A memoir*. Sydney: Hodder Australia.

Cloud, W., & Granfield, W. (2009). Conceptualising recovery capital: Expansion of a theoretical construct. *Substance Use and Misuse, 42*, 1971–1986.

Ferguson, M. (2005). *Smacked: A harrowing story of addiction and survival*. Cape Town, South Africa: Oshun.

Forrell, S., & Gray, A. (2009). Outreach legal services to people with complex needs: What works? *Justice Issues, Paper 12*. Sydney: Law and Justice Foundation of New South Wales. Retrieved February 26, 2014, from http://www.lawfoundation.net.au/ljf/site/articleIDs/69EBF819BDD1BB8BCA25766A0082208C/$file/JI12_Complex_Needs_web.pdf

Frey, J. (2003). *A million little pieces*. New York: First Anchor Books.

Godley, S. H., Smith, J. E., Meyers, R. J., & Godley, M. D. (2001). Adolescent community reinforcement approach (A-CRA). In D. W. Springer & A. Rubin (Eds.), *Substance abuse treatment for youth and adults*. Hoboken, NJ: John Wiley & Sons.

Gray, J. P. (2001). *Why our drug laws have failed and what we can do about: A judicial indictment of the war on drugs*. Philadelphia: Temple University Press.

Holden, K. (2005). *In my skin: A memoir*. Melbourne, Australia: Text Publishing.

Jensen, E. L., Gerber, J., & Mosher, C. (2004). Social consequences of the war on drugs: the legacy of failed policy. *Criminal Justice Policy Review, 15*(1), 100–121.

MacDonald, R., Shildrick, T., Webster, C., & Simpson, D. (2005). Growing up in poor neighbourhoods: The significance of class and place in the extended transitions of "socially excluded" young adults. *Sociology, 39*(5), 873–891.

Newburn, T. (1999). Drug prevention and youth justice: Issues of philosophy, practice and policy. *The British Journal of Criminology, 39*(4), 609–624.

Priebe, S., & Matanov, A. (n.d.). *Good practice in mental health care for socially marginalized people in Europe: Findings from the PROMO Project*. Retrieved

February 26, 2014, from http://www.tnn.ie/PROMO%20Information%20 Sheet.pdf

Reuter, P. (2013). Why has US drug policy changed so little over 30 years? *Crime and Justice, 42*(1), 75–140.

Rowe, J. (2002). Heroin epidemic! Drugs and moral panic in the western suburbs of Melbourne 1995–6. *Just Policy, 27.*

St Christopher House. (2007). *Access for marginalized immigrants and refugees: Issues, barriers and skills required for front line workers.* Retrieved February 26, 2014, from https://www.google.com.au/url?sa=t&rct=j&q=&esrc=s&source =web&cd=3&cad=rja&ved=0CDsQFjAC&url=http%3A%2F%2Fwww. stchrishouse.org%2Fmodules%2FImageAV%2Flib%2FgetImage. php%3FkoId%3D18221&ei=Us4NU-XdPMOGkAXBooCABg&usg= AFQjCNEeY3K-MnOGvhV7paqf4t84gM4d9Q&sig2=xz1mwIYoYnsgAyt ffd07lQ&bvm=bv.61965928,d.dGI

Ungar, M. (2013). The impact of youth-adult relationships on resilience. *International Journal of Child, Youth and Family Studies, 3*, 328–336.

Victorian Premier's Drug Advisory Council (PDAC). (1996). *Drugs and our community: Report of the premier's drug advisory council.* Melbourne, Australia: Victorian Government.

World Health Organisation. (1986). *The Ottawa Charter for health promotion.* Retrieved from www.who.int/healthpromotion/conferences/previous/ottawa/ en/#

8

Conclusion

I have used this book to investigate how some young people come to experience problematic substance use. The research began questioning two dominant assumptions. The first assumption was that drug use inevitably leads to problematic drug use. The second assumption was that young people are unable to make sensible or rational decisions about their drug use. There have been various Australian studies that have examined youth with substance abuse issues, and this research has typically focused on identifying risk and protective factors (Hawkins et al. 1992; Loxley et al. 2004). This information is very useful, but keeps the discussion of young people's drug use contained to these factors alone, which overlooks how these factors came to be at play in young people's lives and the interception of structural issues—namely, poverty—that create and exacerbate "risks". Focus on risk and protective factors constrains the capacity to understand *why* some young people find drugs so appealing at such a young age. One aim of this research has been to fill this gap.

Chapter 1 began with case studies of Larry, Jerry and Lisa. Their biographies showed different pathways into problematic substance use. This had led me to wonder if problematic drug use was simply "bad luck", so I explored what the "drug problem" was. In doing this, it became clear

© The Author(s) 2016
K. Daley, *Youth and Substance Abuse*,
DOI 10.1007/978-3-319-33675-6_8

that most people who use drugs do so without having a problem, so the assumption that drug use always causes problematic drug use was flawed.

The assumption that young people are not making reasoned decisions when they choose to use drugs was also challenged. While those with problematic use did appear to be engaged in reckless drug-using behaviour, closer attention showed that they were actually making "situated choices" regarding their drug use. Critics of the normalisation thesis (Shiner and Newburn 1997) seemed correct when they said that normalisation theories oversimplified young people's drug use. It became clear that young people with problematic drug use did have very different drug use patterns from their more "mainstream" peers, but this was because they were a very different cohort of young people. As I started to untangle some of the nuances, I sought to explore how it was that young people travelled their path into problematic use and drew on the theoretical concept of "situated choices" to understand this. To do this, it was necessary to work backwards and look at young people who had experienced problematic use and trace their biographies. I undertook life-history interviews with 61 young people aged 14 to 24 accessing a variety of youth AOD services across Victoria.

When I met the participants, many of them were homeless and had been living lives that were full of risk. Crime and sex work were accepted as ways of raising money. Life on the streets exposed them to considerable danger. Violence, overdose and the ever-present threat of sexual assault punctuated young people's descriptions of their lives. On the streets, their youth and absence of support left them vulnerable to predators. We learned that these young people's drug use had little to do with pleasure; rather participants wanted "to stop feeling".

In Chap. 3, I explored their early childhood. The chapter revealed that the young people's developmental years had been characterised by poverty, patchy schooling and family dysfunction. Half of them had been in state care and some of the others should have been.

While it was apparent that these young people had lived lives that were very different from their mainstream peers, it was unclear how they transitioned from childhood trauma to substance abuse. In Chap. 4, we saw that there was diversity in young people's pathways, but there were several features that were commonly "in the mix". The triple disconnection from school, family and home was a critical juncture that was significant in the transition from substance use to substance abuse.

Thus far in the book the focus had been on *how* young people developed problematic substance use. I then turned my attention to offer explanations for *why* this had occurred. To do this, I examined women and men separately. In Chap. 5, we saw that young women's experiences of sexual abuse and abandonment often led to dissociation and self-injury. They used cutting as a way of managing their intense emotional pain, before graduating to substance abuse.

Chapter 6 showed that the young men interviewed had very clear ideas about what working-class hegemonic masculinity expected of them. The realisation in their early teens that they had no place in the labour force saw them redefine this notion of masculinity to one of machismo, which celebrated crime and drug use. However, this style of masculinity dictated that men were never to be emotional or vulnerable. Young men masked their emotional turmoil with the presentation of a "front stage" self. In turn, young men found that drugs were an effective way of suppressing their emotions.

Both young men and women were using drugs "to stop feeling", but their drug use had created other problems in their lives. Chapter 7 showed the participants' attempts at "moving on" from substance abuse. Young people's aspirations for their futures were not grand; however, they faced many barriers in the path to achieving them.

Limitations

There are, of course, methodological limitations to this study. The first pertains to the generalisability of the findings. When this study began, there was no data available on the number of young people accessing youth AOD services in Victoria. It was estimated that there were approximately 600–650 young people at any point in time. This estimation was based on the distribution of funds with a caseload of approximately 16 clients for each funded position in the state. This estimation had been the general figure used in the sector for some time. Recently, there has been a census of young people accessing youth AOD services (Kutin et al.

2014). Thirty-six of 48 youth AOD service providers took part (75 per cent) and produced had 1000 completed surveys and a response rate of 84 per cent. Therefore, the sample in this study is comprised of less than 5 per cent of the population.

As much as possible, the sample was stratified for gender and geographic location. Nonetheless, when looking at subgroups the numbers are small. Future studies would be strengthened by having a larger sample size or by looking exclusively at particular subpopulations. It is difficult to verify the validity of data collected in qualitative studies, although the dominance of some themes (e.g. self-injury) suggests that the findings are reliable. Further, the findings in this study are consistent with those of the aforementioned census, which helps to triangulate the research findings.

An important qualification is that the current study only recruited those in treatment. As was noted in the previous chapter, many young people only entered treatment by some sort of fortuitous happenstance, including involvement in the criminal justice system. This suggests that there are probably significant numbers of young people who may be in need of treatment but who are not accessing it. Therefore, it is unknown whether the findings of this study reflect the pathways of all young people experiencing problematic substance use in Victoria. It seems probable that there is an under-representation of young women in services as they are a "hidden" population by virtue of the fact that they are less likely to come into contact with the courts or police and often using with an older partner who is not eligible for access to youth services. The women in youth AOD treatment have more severe presentations on all measures except involvement with crime, and this may well be because they receive access to intervention only when their drug use and/or other associated issues become very severe (Daley and Kutin 2013).

The young people in this study were also all English-speaking. Cultural minorities remain under-represented in all youth AOD services. It is likely that some groups, particularly those who immigrated to Australia as refugees, have a very different pathway into problematic substance use, though it is reasonable to believe that trauma and instability would remain consistent themes. Another minority group who are under-represented here are young people from minority groups of either sexuality and/or gender. While it is known that they have a higher prevalence of drug use (Leonard et al. 2010), they are not proportionately represented in the service system. Future studies could undertake targeted-sampling to gain greater representation of these groups. Or at the least, be examining why this group are not engaged with services.

A final limitation pertains to the possibility of under-reporting. It is possible that some people were guarded about some aspects of their lives. This limitation is compounded by the fact that some of the issues that I have explored (e.g. sexual abuse, cutting) are stigmatised and young people may not disclose them. This is especially true for males who may feel reticent about disclosing sexual abuse and/or cutting. One way around this might be to spend more time getting to know participants or perhaps by undertaking follow-up interviews.

Policy and Practice

The aim of this study was to provide a detailed account of young people's pathways into problematic substance use. The intention was to provide important evidence that can be used to guide effective policy. It is imperative to understand young people's pathways into problematic substance use in order to design prevention programmes, as well as to design programmes that assist people with substance abuse issues. Having mapped out these pathways, much was learned. What was striking was that the young people had experienced so many significant events. Sexual abuse was compounded by abandonment and homelessness. Grief was trapped in masculinities where violence and machismo were more normal than school or dinner. It was a constellation of compounding traumas that led to problematic drug use. Therefore, effective prevention and intervention initiatives need to be tailored accordingly. At a broader level, structural factors need to be redressed. These young people presented to treatment many years after their problems began and after having much contact with many services and systems along the way.

The research findings indicate eight points relevant for policy and practice:

- Need for early intervention that fosters resilience
- Improved access to services
- Increased capacity in schools for youth "at risk"
- Consideration of the different needs of men and women when designing programmes
- Increased focus on family interventions
- Increased resourcing in the care and protection system
- Availability of safe and secure housing for all young people
- Changes in the delivery of funding and policy structures.

Substance abuse generally did not become an issue until participants had left school. This was usually in their early to mid-teens. However, it was clear that their pathway to problematic substance use was being paved much earlier than this. Young people's biographies of early childhood demonstrated that poverty, abuse, neglect and parental substance abuse were more common than not. This information suggests that it would be possible to develop targeted early-intervention initiatives. The family is often the source of a young person's troubles, and parents may not disclose the issues that their children are experiencing. Thus, other adults in young people's lives need to be aware that responsibility may lie with them.

In identifying who would most benefit from early-intervention initiatives, there are some young people who are fairly obvious targets—for example, those involved in the care and protection system—but in other cases it is less obvious. One group where some of the young people may be "at risk" are those who have attended three or more schools. When schools enrol students who have attended many different schools, this could be used as a referral opportunity to the school welfare team. In addition, young people at risk of being expelled from school, or who are experimenting with alcohol and other drugs, may be part of the "at risk" population, where some preliminary investigation might be warranted.

These early warning signs also point to the possibility of targeted prevention programmes. These programmes would need to focus not only on "risks" but also on building resilience. Priority should be given to developing strategies that reduce the need to use drugs as a way of "stopping emotions". The role of family in young people's lives is always central. Including families in prevention and early-intervention programmes is likely to lead to greater efficacy and sustainability. The efficacy of any intervention, however, will be influenced by its accessibility. This appears to be a shortcoming in the current system, with many teenagers not knowing about services.

It has been shown that the young people in this study benefitted from engaging with AOD services. However, we have also seen that many stumbled upon a youth AOD service by a stroke of luck, or some other seemingly accidental circumstance. This makes it likely that there are many more young people in need of these services than we are currently aware of. It is going to be challenging to "promote" services to young people more effectively yet at the same time not to "promote" drug use. This must be balanced against the risks of leaving teenagers with substance abuse issues to face their demons on their own. Models of "assertive outreach" need to be widespread. Outposts in places such as child protection residential units, youth justice offices, schools and mental health services would be a feasible step.

There were gender differences in young people's pathways, which is a relatively undocumented phenomenon. Recently there has been some attention given to it in the Victorian media (Stark 2013), though there has been no investment of funds or commitment to programmatic responses. Young women need services that are equipped to work with their specific needs and to engage them in services earlier and this is not unique to Australia (Simpson and McNulty 2008).

Regardless of how dysfunctional many of the families were, all of the young people wanted a greater sense of family connectedness. Sometimes this is not possible. Some participants were aware that it had been necessary to be removed from their parents' care. Unfortunately, they often went from a dysfunctional family to a care system where there was no stability. This happens when teenagers are housed with other volatile young people who have considerable needs of their own. Greater attention to providing a sense of family towards connectedness would better cater for the needs of vulnerable teenagers and work reducing the rates of intergenerational contact with child protection systems.

More than half of the participants had been involved in the state-care and protection system. Of those who had not, many should have been. There is no escaping the need for a state-care system. However, there are many shortcomings in the current delivery of services, particularly for those children and young people placed into residential care. The structure of the Victorian Child Protection system is reasonable. However, the model of residential units is problematic because of factors such as "contamination" between children. If risky behaviours are a normalised part of the culture for the residents, the likelihood that new residents will take part in such risky behaviour is heightened. Young people in these units are often so troubled that it is unlikely that they will recover unless they are provided with one-to-one care.

Residential units were but one part of a child protection issue. The most significant and inescapable fact is that there is a severe shortage of funding. While the structure of the system is reasonable, it is too poorly resourced to run efficiently. More young men in this study graduated from child protection into youth justice, than graduated from secondary school. Investing in better care of children in Out of Home Care is essential to prevent them from experiencing the multiple issues that the young people in this study faced. Foster care has better outcomes than residential care, but this is likely to be at least partly explained by the fact that children placed in residential care are those who are the most traumatised (Commission for Children and Young People 2015). It would follow logically from this that it is this group who also need the most investment and intensive support, which residential care is not equipped to deliver.

Finally, 90 per cent of the young people in this research had been homeless. It was clear that this contributed to mental health issues, disengagement from school and an increase in drug use consistent with the findings of others (Mendes et al., 2014; Percora et al. 2009). Once young people were homeless, addressing any of these issues became impossible because the immediate need for both shelter and safety were not met. While housing will not solve these issues, it will prevent them from getting worse. It has been established that the longer one is homeless, the greater the likelihood that they will remain homeless in the long term (Chamberlain et al. 2007; Johnson and Chamberlain 2008a, 2008b). To curb this, greater housing options with security and stability need to be directed to homeless youth. Similarly, workers need to enact assertive outreach programmes to find the young people sleeping in squats who are unaware of youth services.

This book has demonstrated that there are multiple interconnected issues which lead to poor outcomes for young people. It is established that holistic approaches to a client's needs garner better treatment outcomes (Bruun and Mitchell 2012; Godley et al. 2001); nonetheless services often do not work together well. This is largely due to the distribution of funding for different services coming from different government departments. A housing department is responsible for addressing homelessness and a department of health to address mental health and substance use. A justice department might also need to be involved. Then the departments of both education and social services also have a role. The dilemma is that when there so many departments that have a role, none appear to have *responsibility*. Is the implication that it is the individual's responsibility? To focus on one issue at a time: the housing department will see you when you have reduced your substance use; the substance abuse service will see you when you have addressed your mental health issues. The judge will grant you parole when you have a permanent address … and on it goes.

The issues these young people faced were not individual ones discrete from one another. They were causes of significant structural issues that interconnect each of the above departments. The issue was not an individual or family one; it was a social one. More specifically, it was primarily a consequence of poverty. Certainly, redressing this complicated departmental approach would require significant restructuring of the current system. However, there is no alternate way that can achieve genuinely holistic care and best outcomes for young people.

The central argument of this book has been that problematic drug use is a consequence of chronic trauma and disadvantage that has been left unattended. The structures which constrained my participants' options—an education system which had rejected them, dysfunctional families, and a state-care system that failed to provide adequate care for children—meant that they were making "situated choices" but in very dire circumstances. They also had not had the resources to deal with intense emotional pain; thus they used drugs to stop feeling. As Mary said: "If people are happy with reality, they don't try to escape from it all the time".

These young people's hopes for their futures were not radical. Their aspirations of having employment, a home and a family, while seemingly ordinary, spoke of their appreciation of what most people take for granted but what they themselves had never had: stability. This book began with a diverse collection of narratives; however, as more depth was revealed, their diversity faded and their similarities were revealed. These similarities are important as it is these similarities that keep them "on the outside".

The 61 young men and women in this study each had their own story, but collectively they also told a story. Their collective story made clear that problematic drug use was a consequence of trauma and disadvantage that was left without care.

References

Bruun, A., & Mitchell, P. (2012). *A resource for strengthening therapeutic practice frameworks in youth AOD services.* Melbourne: Youth Support and Advocacy Service.

Chamberlain, C., Johnson, G., & Theobald, J. (2007). *Homelessness in Melbourne: Confronting the challenge.* Melbourne: RMIT Publishing.

Commission for Children and Young People. (2015). *"...as a good parent would ..." Inquiry into the adequacy of the provision of residential care services to Victorian children and young people who have been subject to sexual abuse or sexual exploitation whilst residing in residential care.* Melbourne: Commission for Children and Young People.

Daley, K., & Kutin, J. (2013). *Young women in youth alcohol and other drug services.* Melbourne, Australia: Youth Support + Advocacy Service.

Godley, S. H., Smith, J. E., Meyers, R. J., & Godley, M. D. (2001). Adolescent community reinforcement approach (A-CRA). In D. W. Springer & A. Rubin (Eds.), *Substance abuse treatment for youth and adults.* Hoboken, NJ: John Wiley & Sons.

Hawkins, J. D., Catalano, R. F., & Miller, J. Y. (1992). Risk and protective factors for alcohol and other drug problems in adolescence and early adulthood: Implications for substance abuse prevention. *Psychological Bulletin, 112*(1), 64–105.

Johnson, G., & Chamberlain, C. (2008a). From youth to adult homelessness. *Australian Journal of Social Issues, 43*(4), 563–582.

Johnson, G., & Chamberlain, C. (2008b). Homelessness and substance abuse: Which comes first? *Australian Social Work, 61*(4), 342–356.

Kutin, J., Bruun, A., Mitchell, P., Daley, K., & Best, D. (2014). *Statewide youth needs census 2013 technical report: Young people in AOD services in Victoria, Victoria-wide results*. Melbourne, Australia: Youth Support + Advocacy Service.

Leonard, W., Marshall, D., Hillier, L., Mitchell, A., & Ward, R. (2010). *Beyond homophobia: Meeting the needs of same sex attracted and gender questioning (SSAGQ) young people in Victoria*. Monograph Series Number 75. The Australian Research Centre in Sex, Health & Society, La Trobe University: Melbourne.

Loxley, W., Toumbourou, J. W., Stockwell, T., Haines, B., Scott, K., Godfrey, C., et al. (2004). *The prevention of substance use, risk and harm in Australia: A review of the evidence*. Canberra, Australia: Australian Government Department of Health and Ageing.

Mendes, P., Baidawi, S., & Snow, P. (2014). Young people transitioning from out-of-home care: A critical analysis of leaving care policy, legislation and housing support in the Australian state of Victoria. *Child Abuse Review, 23*(6), 402–414.

Percora, P. J., White, C. R., Jackson, L. J., & Wiggins, T. (2009). Mental health of current and former recipients of foster care: A review of recent studies in the USA. *Child and Family Social Work, 14*(132), 146.

Shiner, M., & Newburn, T. (1997). Definitely, maybe not: The normalisation of recreational drug use amongst young people. *Sociology, 31*(3), 511–529.

Simpson, M., & McNulty, J. (2008). Different needs: Women's drug use and treatment in the UK. *International Journal of Drug Policy, 19*(2), 169–175.

Stark, J. (2013). *Girls much more likely to suffer abuse, violence and trauma, study finds*. The Sunday Age, p. 5. Retrieved June 28, 2014, from http://www.theage.com.au/victoria/girls-much-more-likely-to-suffer-abuse-violence-and-trauma-study-finds-20131116-2xnrb.html

Index

© The Author(s) 2016
K. Daley, *Youth and Substance Abuse*,
DOI 10.1007/978-3-319-33675-6